About the Author

Daniel Barthold was born in 1983 in Hildesheim (Germany) and grew up in the Hamburg Metropolitan Region. After graduating in International Management he received his M.Sc. in Sports Management in 2009 at Bond University (Australia).

He has written many features about football but also covered ice hockey, handball and other sports in Germany and the United Kingdom. For nearly ten years Daniel Barthold worked for a sports betting consultancy in London where he resides since 2010.

Travelling and association football are his main passion particularly for the German football club Sankt Pauli. Over the years, he started a quest to watch at least one football match in every European country and he is a keen sports traveller in North and South America with a great interest in rivalries.

Sunset in São Paulo

Daniel Barthold

Sunset in São Paulo

Olympia Publishers
London

A CIP catalogue record for this title is
available from the British Library.

ISBN: 978-1-78830-967-7

First Published in 2021

Olympia Publishers
Tallis House
2 Tallis Street
London
EC4Y 0AB

Printed in Great Britain

Dedication

Dedicated to my wife Mônica and our daughter Victoria

In memory of Diego Armando Maradona, Robert Enke, Gary Speed and the Chapecoense football team of 2016

Acknowledgements

I want to thank my wife, Mônica, for her patience and endurance during so many meaningless lower league football fixtures she had to attend with me. Te amo.

A special thanks to my grandma, Irmgard Mallwitz, who passed away in November 2019 at ninety-nine years of age. Her life stories were invaluable and taught me a lot about humility.

Thanks to my sister, Sara, my mum, Liane, and my dad, Hartwig, for all the support.

There have been many travel companions on my journeys. Old friends, new friends, co-workers and random conversation partners on trains, planes, buses and in work offices. It would be impossible to recall them all but thanks to Nikolaus Wiedecke, Anton Shchotkin, Ayumu Yorozui, Roman Fischer, Kerim Sijercic, Andres Pastor, Brian Therkelsen, Benjamin Schomburg, Marco Runig, Torsten Pauly, Niall Guinness, Uwe Mengs, Ralf Bosse, Uli Hesse, Milena Ružić, Tony Bloom, Matty Bosnjak, Chris Moore, Christian Goring, Matt Owton, Julian Schmidt, Tankred Heimerl.

A big thank you also to the National Archive in Warsaw and the Majdanek State Museum in Poland for providing the digital image from barrack 44 at Majdanek Concentration Camp.

Contents

Chapter 1
Fascination stadium hopping

I remember my first football visit outside my home country Germany very well. It was a weekend in Helsinki in September 1999. Germany beat Finland 2–1 in qualifying group 3 for the European Championships 2000 at the Olympic Stadium in front of 20,184 spectators. I recall it to have been a sunny few days in the Finnish capital and that lovely late summer climate in Scandinavia. My dad and I visited the Sibelius Monument, the Helsinki Cathedral, the Parliament House and enjoyed the sun in one of the city's parks.

The Olympic Stadium back then was a fairly big oval which certainly had its charm and although it has been refurbished over the years, when I see it on television now it is still quite similar to the time when I was there—I think new seats and a new roof have been built during its renovation in 2019.

It is fair to say that it was a perfect start to become a so-called 'stadium hopper' or 'groundhopper' but obviously, at the time I had not heard this term and I was far away from 'ticking off' football grounds on a European or even worldwide scale. Helsinki was an important starter though due to the success of the trip. From then on, I would start visiting international fixtures on an annual basis with my dad and whenever it was possible to see a new stadium we went for it.

In 2000 it was Liége at the Euros, 2001 White Hart Lane in north-east London and Hampden Park, 2002 Celtic Park in Glasgow, 2003 the Estadio Bernabéu in Madrid and finally 2004 when I visited the Euros with a friend in Portugal. The tournament would become a very important chapter in my 'groundhopping career' as I met a few stadium hoppers personally. They told me that they were off to Guimarães on the quest to see every ground of the tournament. It was the first time that I thought that this kind of idea would suit me very well. I love sports statistics so to make a list with all the fixtures I had attended and set targets for future stadiums to see was very appealing to me. There was a German documentary once about a group of football fans who travelled to the Czech Republic to attend several lower tier matches and a well-known Nottingham Forest supporter who lives in Duisburg (near Düsseldorf). Ebby Kleinrensing is his name who as far as I know still flies over to Nottingham regularly to see Forest play. The documentary has pretty much cult status amongst German football fans but it was a bit early for me to really get into the topic as it was aired first in the late 90's on Germany's, back-then, biggest sports channel DSF. I just thought it was a very funny and entertaining story on these crazy football travellers. However, it was the Euro 2004 that made me start listing stadiums and matches I had attended in a 'more professional' manner. It was the starting point of hundreds of football trips with every match having its own story. One groundhopper made a very interesting comment about this extraordinary passion. He said: 'Groundhopping is a mixture of several addictions: it is a football addiction, an extreme desire of wanderlust and it is also a passion for collecting. Let's say you have ticked off 17 out of 18 Czech Premier League grounds, then you obviously want to make the last missing stadium certainly as well'. I fully agree on his statement, but it includes so much more which I have realized quite clearly on my travels. It's the history and customs of a country, the different fan bases and rivalries, the various mentalities and also the view of the people on being German. It is a journey that can probably never be completely fulfilled—it is impossible to see every ground in the world—but it offers very valuable lessons and experiences that I will tell in this book.

Chapter 2
My home football club

I have been living in London for ten years now and spent some time in Ireland, New Zealand, and the United States as well. I graduated from Bond University in Australia on top so although I grew up in the Hamburg area, I have not been 'home' too much in the last ten to fifteen years. I was born in Hildesheim (near Hannover) and moved just outside Hamburg with my parents and my sister in 1990. Football has been an important part of my life probably since I was five. Playing football in the backyard with my dad, watching matches on television or collecting the famous Panini stickers for major tournaments really defined me growing up in a pretty easy environment—it is fair to say that I had a nice childhood. I joined my local football club TSV Buchholz 08 when I was in school and the World Cup 1990 I will never forget. I do remember my first day at school and other early events. The fall of the Wall I do not have any recollections of, but the World Cup in Italy is still very fresh in my mind. I remember my dad getting excited when Germany beat Yugoslavia 4-1, the late Colombia goal in Germany's third group game, the legendary battle against Holland in the round of the last sixteen including the disgusting scenes between Frank Rijkaard and Rudi Völler, the penalty shoot-out against England in the semis and of course, Andi Brehme's penalty in the World Cup Final. All these events I can recall as a six-year-old boy sitting in front of the television.

It really accelerated my passion for football.

The Euros 1992 were another major tournament that excited me as a young fan. I remember crying when Holland beat Germany 3-1 in the group stages and my mum getting angry and telling me off. She said that we will not watch football again if I cry when the opponent scores a goal. It makes me smile when I think about it now because my passion for the German national team really has gone down to an extremely moderate level over the years. Especially some nationalist or even racist chants from parts of fan bases (not only in Germany) had put me off the older I got so crying when Germany concedes a goal is something I would never do these days. Nevertheless, I can't deny that I follow each and every major tournament very closely and those summer fests every two years are still something I always look forward to.

My real passion though—like for most football fans—is my home football club. In the early 90's my dad and I used to attend fixtures of both Hamburg-based teams, Hamburger SV (HSV) and FC St. Pauli. In the mid-90's HSV used to be somewhere mid-table in the Bundesliga and St. Pauli managed to play in the top tier for two years and were fighting against relegation as expected.

Hamburg's Volksparkstadion was a stadium not very close from the city centre in the Stellingen area which really needed some major refurbishment. The stands were far from the pitch with the obligatory running track and I don't recall the ground to be particularly noisy at the time. I kind of denied it for many years but at some point I remembered that I once had a HSV hat that I used to wear when I was at Volkspark. At the same time though, I bought my first St. Pauli scarf when I attended fixtures at their Millerntorstadium. I guess when you are twelve years old you just don't think too much about rivalries and I sort of supported both teams. This changed in 1997. St. Pauli were relegated back to Bundesliga 2 and still, I decided to buy my first season ticket at the arguably smaller club whereas Hamburg stayed in Germany's top flight. I am still not 100% sure what caused this decision to support a club that simply struggled to perform well considering my early love of football. In the end, as a young teenager I think it must have been the atmosphere at Millerntor. It did not matter if it was at the queue to get a fresh Bratwurst, waiting in line to go to the toilet or simply the supporters who were sitting next to my dad and me, everyone was relaxed and friendly. At HSV, often people were swearing badly or pushed you around when getting to and from the stadium. Also, it seemed inconvenient to get to the Volksparkstadion every fortnight, Millerntorstadium was right in the heart of Hamburg and without really knowing an exact event of my decision I started attending St. Pauli matches as a season ticket holder.

Inevitably, away games were an option too at some point and my first ever match on the road was at FC Gütersloh in 1998, a small club near Bielefeld. St. Pauli—considering its limited success and empty trophy cabinet—have a pretty big fan base and when Jens Scharping scored a penalty in the 90th minute to make it 1–1 it was a happy afternoon. Yes, St. Pauli fans are generally happy with a draw which tells you quite a lot about the success of the club…

My mum was nice enough to allow away trips by myself even at a fairly young age of fifteen or sixteen. I remember traveling to Bochum some 3.5 hours from Hamburg and even further to Mainz in the south-west of Germany on a Friday night respectively. I left Hamburg Central station straight after school and took one of the fast trains. I remember being worried to not miss the night train back north as I only had a limited amount of money available and going to a football match it is normal to meet a few rather strange people or at least supporters who had way too much to drink. It is quite an experience as a teenager to stand in a full away end such as the one that Friday night in Bochum with some intense chants and seeing these die-hard supporters on the terraces. Two incidents I recall quite clearly despite this being roughly 20 years ago. Before the match a fan asked me if he could borrow my match ticket for a second. I did not know why he wanted the ticket but I guess his plan was to hand it to someone outside the stadium who did not have access to the away terrace. Naively, I gave him my ticket and he never came back. I need to add that from the early days I have been a very passionate collector of match tickets and it has always been the most important souvenir of matches I attend so it bothered me a lot back then until the day I found a match ticket from the exact same fixture on ebay for under two Euros. It was the first of two incidents where I lost a match ticket which is a pretty good record for someone who has been going to stadiums for nearly thirty years now. The second time I lost a ticket was my fault and I am not entirely sure how it happened. After a 0-0 draw at VfL Osnabrück in 2000 I had a stopover at Bremen Central and decided to buy a sandwich and I think the ticket must have dropped out of my pocket. I was really disappointed in myself considering the mentioned passion for match tickets.

There are countless memories as a St. Pauli supporter and most events in my life are connected to fixtures I either attended or followed from elsewhere in the world. Former East Germany used to be a bit of a danger zone for St. Pauli fans due to the left-right-wing rivalries and some clubs in the east had a rather severe right-wing fan base whereas St. Pauli is known for being left-wing and anti-fascist so when I was a teenager I avoided attending away games in the former GDR. Live games on pay-tv were not that advanced in the late 90's so a number of fixtures I followed via teletext. When we played at VfB Leipzig—today known as Lokomotive Leipzig—I refreshed the teletext as often as I could and it had been 0–0 until the 89th minute, when I refreshed it one more time, it all of a sudden said: VfB Leipzig 2 St. Pauli 0, goals 89', 90'. Such harsh disappointment I experienced quite regularly.

One time we played at Unterhaching in the Munich area and levelled in stoppage time to make it 1–1 just to concede once more a minute later to eventually lose 2–1. Events like this have branded me surely because nowadays, even when St. Pauli are winning 3–0 with say ten minutes left to play I still think we could end up playing 3–3. To be fair, we have improved on that a little bit over the last ten years or so and did not drop points that harshly too often of late.

Just to clarify, I actually enjoy going to eastern Germany nowadays, I remember having some decent night outs in Leipzig, Dresden or Erfurt and there have been some great away wins over there. The infamous 2–0 away win at rivals Rostock and club legend Deniz Naki ramming a St. Pauli flag into the pitch which was quite controversial—including a 'chopping-head-off'-gesture directed at the home fans. That fixture took place in season 2009/2010 when St. Pauli managed to get promoted to the Bundesliga on its 100th birthday. That year the club played its centennial against Celtic Football Club at home in front of a Millerntorstadium being under construction (St. Pauli share a close friendship with Celtic supporters).

A recent memory on the road in eastern Germany was the 2–1 away win at Magdeburg in August 2018. A lovely free-kick by Marvin Knoll secured the victory on match day 1 in a hostile atmosphere.

Very special are obviously the Hamburg derbies against HSV. Hamburger SV are a huge club with a pretty full trophy cabinet but has also struggled in recent years with financial problems and constant deterioration on the pitch which resulted in relegation to the second tier for the first time in their history.

One of the most recent derbies took place on February 20th 2020 at Volksparkstadion in front of 57,000 supporters. A triumphant 2–0 win for St. Pauli which was the second victory over the local rivals in one season. What I will never forget is the celebration in the away end when Sheffield Wednesday loanee Matthew Penney hammered in a great effort from outside the box to make it 2–0 after 29 minutes. It was pure ecstasy on a day when I got up at 3am to catch the 6.50am flight from Heathrow to Hamburg and stress all day due to the intensity of this derby. I flew back to the UK the same day but as you can tell it was all worth it and every football fan would agree that derby days are something special. The Hamburg derby is tense but I would like to add that there are a number of moderate fans in the city who actually like both clubs. This is certainly a scenario that would be unthinkable in Glasgow, Istanbul, Belgrade or Buenos Aires that there is sympathy for the respective arch-rival.

St. Pauli home games are always special as well as being situated right in the heart of the city adjacent to the infamous Reeperbahn. My first season ticket I had was in season 1997/1998 straight after relegation from Germany's top flight and the club back then was in a much worse financial position than these days. The stadium was outdated and the team was Bundesliga 2 average but we can always count on great support and atmosphere. Once we played FSV Mainz 05—actually St. Pauli played them quite often in Bundesliga 2—and scored the winner in stoppage by Turkish midfielder Cem Karaca, a player who was very fast but also equally limited. After the game, none other than Jürgen Klopp, who was a player at Mainz at the time was fuming in a post-match interview that the referee did not have the game under control and called out the reporter for a silly question. Klopp always seemed to struggle dealing with defeats and this one was tough with that last minute equalizer. I love stoppage time winners and I recall visiting my grandma the following day who used to live two hours from Hamburg in between Hannover and Braunschweig and my mood could not have been better. It is usually not recommended to wear a St. Pauli jersey in other cities—at least back then I did not do it much outside match days—but that day I just felt like doing it no matter what and quite frankly, these days I would do it anyway, it is just different when you are fifteen years old in a different city.

Another outstanding memory was the 2–1 victory over Bayern Munich who were reigning FIFA Club World Champions in 2002. After an extremely unexpected promotion to the Bundesliga in 2001 St. Pauli finished hopelessly bottom of the table with a very limited but courageous side and that mid-week night at Millerntor was special. St. Pauli scored two goals within three minutes in the first half and managed to get the 2–1 lead over the line. Bayern's players certainly were not keen on playing in such a ramshackle stadium with dressing rooms known as 'the filthiest in Germany'. Since the stadium has been completely renovated it actually took away a bit of St. Pauli's home advantage. Nowadays, opponents love to play at St. Pauli due to its location and it's much improved facilities. Especially smaller clubs see St. Pauli away as one of their season highlights.

I was fortunate enough not to have had many violent encounters as a St. Pauli fan. Some like us in Germany, some really don't. Since the 1990s, Hansa Rostock have been one of our arch-rivals with some very tense clashes. If I had to pick my personal Millerntor highlight it would probably be our 3–2 win over Rostock in 2009. St. Pauli were 2–0 down after six minutes and at half-time the away end erupted like a volcano with flares all over the place. Back then manager and club legend Holger Stanislawski said after the game: 'When someone lays a fire in your living room you take it personal'. St. Pauli ended up winning 3–2 and Canadian international Junior Hoilett, former Blackburn Rovers, QPR and currently Cardiff City, played one of his best games in the brown and white jersey (St. Pauli's colours). Hoilett was one of these players not good enough for the big stage but too talented for St. Pauli to stay at the club for longer than one season. I do remember a second great performance of his when St. Pauli beat Alemannia Aachen 3–1 away at their legendary 'Tivoli'—a stadium that had sadly been demolished in 2011.

I am sure every football fan can connect life events to certain results and fixtures of the club he supports. It is the same with me, of course. The day before my graduation exams at school in 2003 I decided to pack away my books and take the train to Ahlen near Dortmund for a crucial relegation battle fixture on a fairly grey Sunday. Unfortunately, St. Pauli lost 3–2 and eventually got relegated to the third tier. The three hour one way train journey gave me the chance to study but the narrow defeat still overshadowed everything despite the fact that I graduated satisfactory from school to later join the university where I had a similar experience in 2007. I was having my final exams in Spanish that week—a language I had to take as part of my business degree and most of my colleagues had been struggling to make too much progress so it was basically all about just passing the oral exam in that language. Also that week St. Pauli were playing at Rot-Weiss Erfurt in Bundesliga 3 de facto securing promotion to the second tier after a four year absence with a win. I was lucky enough to have a car at the time and spontaneously decided on matchday to drive the five hours down to Erfurt. It was a close call knowing the importance of passing the exam at university but three points in the league were so important that I simply had to go. I left the house about five hours before kick-off so I knew it would have been tough to make it on time. I expected it to be a quiet Sunday on the road but due to construction on Hamburg's freeway I was extremely late and arrived inside the stadium in Erfurt roughly five minutes before half-time. Luckily, I did not seem to have missed too much as the score was 0–0. I usually follow St. Pauli in the away end but this time I ended up at Erfurt's main stand which actually offered me a much better view on the pitch and also the vocal and full away end on the other side of the ground. St. Pauli won the game 3–0 in the end after a strong second half performance and got promoted one week later at home following a 2–2 draw against Dynamo Dresden. It was the second of three major promotion celebrations I was fortunate to experience. As St. Pauli are unlikely to win any trophies any time soon promotion and derby wins are pretty much the only big achievements we have. In 2001, St. Pauli beat Nuremberg away 2–1 to secure the most unexpected promotion in club history—that season St. Pauli were expected to get relegated due to the fact that we just about stayed up the season before on last match day with a goal in stoppage time by Marcus Marin. Due to the communion of my cousin near Bielefeld I was not able to attend the match in Nuremberg—a stadium I have visited quite often—but I joined the promotion celebrations that evening in Hamburg when the players returned.

In 2003, St. Pauli got relegated from Bundesliga 2 to Bundesliga 3 after an awful season—so we are talking straight relegations from the Bundesliga to the third tier within two successive seasons—and the club spent four years in the third tier which was at the time not considered a professional league. Later on in 2007, the club finally managed to return to Bundesliga 2 with that mentioned draw against Dresden and promotion to the Bundesliga in season 2009/2010 was probably the most talented St. Pauli team I have ever witnessed under club legend Holger Stanislawski's helm. On matchday 33 (out of 34) we played at Fürth near Nuremberg to secure promotion with a win. After a nervy first half and being 1–0 down St. Pauli played a stunning second half in front of roughly 9,000 away supporters to win 4–1 and confirm extensive celebrations that week. It was also one of my last away games before my move to London in October 2010. I left Hamburg with St. Pauli still being in Bundesliga 1 which was quite a big decision for me to make because it meant no more season tickets and not attending fixtures on a regular basis anymore. The last match before leaving Germany was at Hannover 96 on a Friday night which was a great 1–0 win in front of a capacity crowd in Lower Saxony (49,000). St. Pauli soon beat Hamburger SV away which was huge—a game that first got postponed due to the waterlogged pitch which destroyed my travel plans. I eventually managed to attend the rearranged fixture which was a lucky and unexpected derby win by the smallest of margins. Schalke 04 legend Gerald Asamoah scored the only goal against a Hamburg side that had the likes of Ruud van Nistelrooy and Zé Roberto in their squad. Unfortunately, St. Pauli ended up being relegated as they did not win a single match afterwards and the so-called 'derby win curse' was born. In 2018 Hamburg hammered St. Pauli 4–0 in our own backyard but failed to win any matches after that bar one which resulted in HSV to remain in Bundesliga 2 to this day.

Quite an emotional experience was my first match after Hannover 96 and German international goalkeeper Robert Enke took his own life in November 2009. It was the season St. Pauli got promoted but that day we would lose at Augsburg against 10 men despite having a lead. The result was a bit secondarily important because the minute of silence and the video about Enke on the screens were extremely moving. He was an idol for many especially young football supporters and his suicide due to depression was a big shock to Germany's football family and beyond.

Outside Millerntor-Stadion - Home of FC St. Pauli

Hamburg Derby Day: Hamburger SV v FC St. Pauli 0-2, February 2020

Chapter 3
The route is the goal

A very common statement by groundhoppers is that they are restless. Looking at fixtures, planning journeys and researching stadiums are constant tasks. Basically while being on the road to a new ground the planning for the next trip had usually commenced already. The 'getting there' factor of stadium hopping is quite an interesting part of the journey and sometimes even a highlight. Being on the road with a group of people can be very enjoyable and quite an adventure. I remember several trips that were almost more fun than the game itself. The first such experience was the Euro 2004 in Portugal and the journey from Faro to Porto via Lisbon by train and bus. Needless to say that Portugal in June is an excellent holiday destination and getting into Lisbon by train is quite an experience to enter the city and the view from the river Tejo. After attending Sweden v Bulgaria at the Estádio José de Alvalade a friend and I took a night bus from Lisbon to Porto trying to get tickets for Germany v Holland at the lovely Estádio do Dragão. We were driving into the city at about 4am and it was quite a scenery to see the still dark city of Porto with all its old sights for the first time. Due to various circumstances I ended up visiting Porto on three more occasions to see Braga's ground, Boavista's stadium and to meet a friend the day after ticking off Benfica's Estádio da Luz when they played Celtic in the Champions League 2012.

My first organized groundhopping trip was in 2006 after the World Cup in Germany. Being a student it was quite popular at the time to buy a so-called 'Interrail ticket' which allowed the passenger to use most trains on the European network with just one rail ticket. The travel plan I had arranged with a friend of mine from the United States was meeting up in Oslo, Norway and then to travel all the way to the Croatian coast. The route looked amazing on paper but due to various issues and being a 'greenhorn' it was not as easy as I thought. First of all, I failed to double check kick-off times and confirmed fixtures which is something that would never happen to me these days especially when you enter Eastern Europe. We had a whole bunch of matches that had been moved to a different stadium or kick-off time so we missed out plenty of new grounds on that four-week-trip.

In the Copenhagen area, Brøndby's home game had been moved from Sunday to Saturday according to a bartender, a Czech Republic international was played in Teplice although I was sure, it was scheduled to be played in Prague and in Trnava, Slovakia the kick-off time had been moved to an early hour that day which is probably the most annoying news for a stadium hopper. It really was the first experience on such a scale and a very important learning curve for me. In years to come, I did not come across too many postponements that I could have researched better. I once landed in Warsaw just for a taxi driver to tell me that the Legia home match was to be played behind closed doors due to crowd trouble the weekend prior and I had some issues in Scotland here and there as well. A postponement in Inverness due to a flu wave in Aberdeen's squad and an abandoned match in Kilmarnock due to sudden fog in the second half were two of the disappointments in recent years. Despite all that, my motivation to tick off new grounds never ceases to be on my mind and that 'Interrail trip' in 2006 was still a successful one as we saw Vålerenga Oslo, Djurgårdens IF and Örgryte IS in Sweden, Wacker Burghausen in Germany including the Euro qualifier against Ireland in Stuttgart and some ridiculous partying with Irish football fans over two days—Ireland lost that game by the way which did not interrupt their celebrations at all...

We attended the Vienna derby between Austria and Rapid and ticked off the Stadium Maksimir in Zagreb including some relaxed days on the Adriatic Coast. The big problem when your first two stops are Oslo and Stockholm and you are a student is that your bank account empties extremely quickly so Eastern Europe and its low prices were inevitable destinations later on. Prague, Bratislava, Budapest and Zagreb are certainly more affordable locations.

I don't think there is a limit on distances for groundhoppers and I have heard people sitting beyond 48 hours on a bus for some lower league football. I do remember some longer journeys but nothing that really exhausted me. In Chile at the Copa América 2015 it was about a nine hour bus journey, the night train from the beautiful city of Bergen to Oslo was a great experience and there had been some longer same day travel drives to see St. Pauli away such as Kaiserslautern or Augsburg.

At some point it was a close call whether to support my own team on a weekend or seeing new stadiums. One Sunday I was supposed to attend a St. Pauli home match and decided to look up other fixtures abroad. I was still based in Hamburg at the time so the obvious options were Denmark which is about a two and a half hour drive away and the Netherlands roughly three hours by car. After using my beloved teletext again, I saw that

Heerenveen were playing at home in the Eredivisie and decided to go there instead. As it was such a spontaneous decision I did not know that tickets sales had stopped by the time I arrived and after I explained to a security guard that I just travelled four hours he gave me a complimentary ticket which was a nice gesture. It is fair to say that on this day I started prioritizing groundhopping over supporting my own club a little bit at least when it comes to options on which fixtures to attend.

Rarely has there been a situation where I could not attend a match other than a postponement or cancellation of course. There was an incident in Uruguay I will talk about later on but I do recall another scary moment on the way from Seattle to Vancouver in 2005 to attend the international women's friendly between Canada and Germany. Back then, I was doing an English language course in Washington State and took the bus to spend two days in beautiful British Columbia. Upon arrival at the border control in Canada I was not aware that I had to bring a special document with me that was connected to my visa—a so-called 'I-20'—in order to return to the United States. Due to the fact that I did not bring the mentioned document I was not allowed into Canada because I could not have re-entered the US on the way back without the paper I needed. It not only meant that I was stranded at the border, I also needed to find a way to get back to Seattle which was about a two hour drive away. In order to get back into the United States, I had to cross the street from the Canadian border control to the US border. So I walked over to the other side, showed my passport and the police officer asked me how I got here. I mistakenly answered that I took the bus from Seattle but what he wanted to know was how I got from the Canadian border to the US border so what he was expecting to hear was: 'I walked over across the street'. When he asked me a third time I finally understood what he meant and realizing that he got angry put me under pressure and it got a bit tense. I was very fortunate that a driver in a small truck heard that I was about to go back to Seattle and offered me a lift for free. That made the situation much easier for me and we were even able to talk a little bit about 'soccer' on the journey back. I attempted to tick off Canada for a football match once again two weeks later. This time by train and with the required documents on me which was another great learning experience to always carry my documents with me, it seemed like it was not obvious for a 21-year-old like me. The border control at Vancouver station was much smoother and I was finally able to experience this gorgeous city. When I took the taxi to Swangard Stadium, back then home of the Vancouver Whitecaps, the driver was a bit irritated that I travelled all the way from Seattle to see the Whitecaps who at the time played in North America's second tier. Usually, if you visit Vancouver for sports it has to be the Canucks in the National Hockey League which would have been interesting as well, however, my priority was seeing a football match in Canada and the NHL season had not started at the time. As expected, it was a low quality football game between the Whitecaps and Montreal Impact but it felt like a victory that I was able to do it after such a difficult and unsuccessful first attempt to get into Vancouver. And it is a great example that sometimes the journey itself is a highlight. The train journey from Seattle to Vancouver is lovely with some scenic landscape, train tracks close to the water and the Peace Arch on the border which represents the peaceful relationship between Canada and the United States.

Chapter 4
The UEFA Members List

Groundhoppers create their own targets constantly and the list of stadiums they want to see expands on a regular basis really. I often add a stadium immediately after I have seen a ground in a respective country almost without noticing it. When I attended a match in Kerkrade (Netherlands) I straight away added Fortuna Sittard to the list, after I went to Boavista Porto in Portugal I thought a match on the island of Madeira would be nice, in Poznań I decided that Łódź would be another Polish city to see— the list will never be fulfilled entirely it seems. I would say it is difficult to really see a football match in every country in the world especially when having a family and considering the financial part of it, also to complete every league in Europe is difficult with 18 or 20 teams per league. I think that every league has at least two or three rather dull grounds in it so apart from Germany and England where I aim to see all grounds of the first three or four leagues of the pyramid (England obviously having the famous '92'—all stadia of the four leagues from the Premier League down to League Two) I don't think I will complete too many leagues in Europe although, as a groundhopper one can't rule out too much in reality when it comes to setting targets.

A big challenge of mine in recent years has been completing the UEFA Members List which includes the task of seeing one football in each of the current 55 European football member countries. It is a target that started in 1999 when I first attended a match outside my home country Germany and it is an on-going challenge which is close to its conclusion (as of August 2020, I have two countries left in Kazakhstan and Armenia). The first time I realized that I might have a chance to complete this list was probably around 2012 or 2013 but at the time I thought it would be difficult to travel to places like Azerbaijan, Armenia or Kazakhstan. The fact that I have been travelling within Europe extensively for over twenty years now makes me some sort of an expert on transportation and random cities all over the continent. For example, I have been to the North Macedonian capital Skopje twice fairly coincidentally. The first time was to attend a match in North Macedonia in the quite impressive National Arena which also included an interesting taxi ride from Skopje to the Bulgarian capital Sofia. I ended up in Skopje again a few years later when I ticked off Kosovo by watching a league game in the village of Drenas. I once again negotiated a deal with a taxi driver who drove me from Kosovo to Macedonia where I was due to fly back to London from Skopje Airport. I was quite impressed by the landscape and mountain range on the way and Kosovo just building up a little bit of an economy was visible with new stores opening up on the streets and local supermarkets running for the latest member in the UEFA family. Kosovo as a country has tight connections to Albania so loads of Albanian flags were to be seen until I reached the North Macedonian border and eventually Skopje with its nice old town and the Stone Bridge.

Some countries really have surprised me when it comes to hospitality and beautiful landscapes. Georgia is a country that comes to my mind which was once again a place where I hired a driver to save time rather than taking the bus. I landed in Kutaisi with one of the low budget airlines. It felt like a city that more represented the Georgian lifestyle than the big capital Tbilisi. Kutaisi has a small market square, a nice river flowing through the city and compared to western Europe it felt a bit stuck in the 80's or 90's but in a positive way. The place really had a nice pace to it so it calmed me down to some degree in comparison to life in overcrowded London. The three hour drive from Kutaisi and Tbilisi was lovely which included some traditional villages in the hills, some nice mountain ranges and it was a bit like a journey into the past in a country finding a transition from the former Soviet Union to modern day Europe. The Soviet past is still visible but unlike Azerbaijan or Armenia, Georgia has a clear interest to be closer to the European Union. Tbilisi, the Georgian capital, is a busy and quite a polluted city with a beautiful national stadium. It is an oval that reminded me of classic former Eastern European stadiums and it would even fit South America. An old-school vibe, bigger capacity, running track and a long history which one can feel straight away. Georgia is an extremely old country and that was probably what impressed me most and I was pleased by the hospitality because everyone really appreciates when you visit the country. My driver picked me up outside the stadium post-match and drove me back to Kutaisi Airport through the night which was a big help that I could trust someone I just met a few hours ago. Nobody wants to be stranded in the middle of nowhere in a country where not everyone outside the big cities speaks English or German.

There are some countries in Europe that I consider perfect for stadium hopping. Obviously, Germany, France (taking regular strikes aside) or England offer a great rail and road network so it is easy to get from a to b and other countries like Spain or Italy include some decent lifestyle with formidable food options and decent weather. Moreover, I find places like Norway or Switzerland gorgeous countries to hang out in and the landscape is in fact breathtaking. But there are places that are not on everyone's radar that fascinated me in so many ways. I remember an amazing three days on the Faroe Islands located in between Norway and Scotland with some fresh seafood and a lovely climate. Thórshavn is a quiet town and not cheap but the quality of life is tremendously high and I will never forget enjoying trips on the ferry as a young family man.

Also, very fresh in my mind was the Nations' League fixture I attended between the Faroe Islands and Malta. Not necessarily the game itself but the fact that it was the foggiest football match that went ahead without even being in doubt. I mentioned before that I once experienced an abandoned game in Kilmarnock (Scotland) due to fog and I am firmly convinced that it was much foggier in Thórshavn that night which I found out from a taxi driver (of course!) was quite normal over there. Needless to say that getting to the Faroe Islands is not something that I plan every day so it would have been beyond frustrating to see that fixture get called off and it was nice to enjoy the match and a fresh Föroya Bjór, the local beer from Klaksvík.

Another country I have fond memories of is the Ukraine during the Euro 2012. It makes a bigger difference if you have a local tour guide because you simply see more and get to see all the sights without missing out on significant places. In the Ukraine I was happy to travel with a friend from Kiev, a city that surprised me as much as the Belarusian capital Minsk. First of all, the weather is gorgeous in June and there are plenty of great restaurants and bars which completely slammed any stereotype as being not open to tourists or 'the West'. I was particularly impressed by the war museum in Kiev and Minsk—cities I both visited on two separate occasions. I will never forget a room at the museum in Kiev dedicated to Soviet and German soldiers who wrote postcards to their loved ones during the Second World War. That entire room with a fairly high ceiling being covered with postcards and some very emotional and personal messages on it in the midst of one of the deadliest battles of mankind was a very moving experience. It certainly supports my idea of really experiencing a country and its people rather than 'just ticking off' a football ground. The same impression I had when I was in Minsk which is sometimes considered the last dictatorship in Europe. Of course, a tourist never experiences the day-to-day struggles of the population and it is always important to appreciate life in a democracy but the locals in Minsk impressed me. Their English was pretty good and their hospitality really is worth mentioning.

One of my favourite cities in the former Soviet Union is L'viv in western Ukraine not far from the Polish border. I had match tickets for the Euro 2012 group stage fixture between Germany and Denmark and had not done much research on the city of L'viv prior but a local friend from Kiev told me that it is a great city and he was certainly right. The old city is preserved and gives you a great 'breeze of the past' with its market square and restaurants that are evident for the long history of the place. It is fair to say that I started to appreciate Eastern Europe more and more over the years on my quest to visit all the UEFA countries. Prague is probably the most popular due to its location and it is the perfect football city with various clubs in the city, smaller football teams with its traditional football grounds and great Czech food and beer. But it is also the cities just like L'viv that are not on everyone's radar that drew my attention. Riga, Vilnius, Tallinn, Kraków, St Petersburg, Bratislava or Budapest are popular destinations these days but I equally enjoyed Brno, Kiev, Minsk, Skopje, Ljubljana and Sarajevo.

One of the most fascinating places I have ever been is certainly Istanbul. I was lucky enough to visit the city twice, first for the game Turkey against Germany and then later on I visited Beşiktaş' stadium prior to its refurbishment. Unfortunately, there was no game on so I was only able to take some pictures. There is also a term for it, 'ground spotting' means visiting a stadium without seeing an actual match but I would not consider it a stadium that should count on the list, my opinion is that a match has to be attended in order to 'tick off' the ground.

Istanbul has many incredible mosques and markets and entering the city on a boat along the Bosporus is quite an experience. In 2011, on a lovely October day I visited Galatasaray's new arena when Turkey hosted Germany in a European qualifier. The stadium itself is impressive but certainly not unique, the architecture is pretty similar to Arsenal's Emirates Stadium or Benfica's Estádio da Luz. What I will always remember from that night is that the infrastructure had not been fully completed, yet to get to and from the football ground turned out to be a bit of an issue. First of all, the Turkish police decided that visitors had to wait an eternity to get out of the stadium and secondly, the advice was for people who do not speak Turkish, to not walk to the next underground station as it was considered 'not safe'. As it was quite late after the game there were no taxis either so my best shot was to ask the driver of a bus that was supposed to bring a bunch of German fans back to their hotel, for a lift. The bus driver was not too keen but a Borussia Mönchengladbach supporter who was organizing the bus journey said that he might have a seat left and that he would not leave a fellow football fan on a street somewhere on the outskirts of Istanbul. I was happy to give him ten Euros and he handed me a beer—a perfect example of how football fans should treat each other and that this community is very solidary.

Being a groundhopper always includes a constant feeling of wanderlust so it is very important for me to get a vibe of the respective country or city before and after attending a football match. It does not matter if it is a market square, a monument, a cathedral or simply a local bar or restaurant, these locations give a certain feel to the place and 99% of my travels I still remember in detail. The Acropolis in Athens before seeing the Greek national team in Piraeus, the Palace square in St Petersburg before attending the Confederations Cup Final in 2017 or the Red Square in Moscow during the World Cup 2018. Visiting historic places will always be connected to the sports grounds I have on my list. And there are events which are simply unique to my personal travels. I once attended a PAOK home match in Thessaloniki—a very loyal fan base—in one single day. I was flying out of Stansted Airport in the morning and flew back at around ten o'clock in the evening. Upon arrival in Greece a taxi driver told me that the entire city is more or less on strike so only a few restaurants were open and he advised to wait at a certain point outside the stadium in order to get one of the few taxis back to the airport after the match. It is quite an interesting experience to be part of certain issues in a country for at least a few hours simply because I planned on attending a football match. It sometimes includes stressful moments which obviously would not have happened if I stayed at home. However, every event, even negative ones, I appreciate as a learning experience and in the case of Thessaloniki I was at least able to help the struggling economy (on a very low scale though). Travelling to me is a major factor of dismantling stereotypes which is something I have been observing over and over again. At the time, it was said that the Greeks were angry at Germany and the European Union for telling Greece how to spend their money based on the economic downfall. On match day in Thessaloniki I spent a few hours in a bar outside the stadium and as I was ordering drinks in English language the bartender asked me where I was from. I was still confident enough to reveal my German nationality, but I was prepared for a possible heated conversation about current politics in Europe. Instead, the guy was extremely friendly and we just talked about the purpose of my journey. It is a very important lesson never to be prejudgemental and, more importantly, it is crucial to distinguish between decisions and opinions by politicians and the views of the people. I noticed that I have learned that on various trips on the UEFA map. A fairly recent memory is Belarus in 2019—with a layover in Lithuania where I spent a night at Vilnius Airport. Of course, as a tourist you bring money into the country and you will be treated very differently compared to locals who question the government or the working class that does not generate much money in a corrupt economic system. And still, I was impressed how relatively open-minded the people in the Minsk area had been. From an easy entry-process at the border control to English speaking drivers and friendly staff in the hotel—just like Kiev and L'viv it really surprised me positively. And the city of Minsk did not disappoint, a nice old town with a lovely river running through and one of the most impressive war museums I have ever seen. The trip included a taxi ride to Borisov for the European qualifier Belarus against Northern Ireland in a UFO-style stadium in the middle of a forest. Quite a bizarre setting and once again, I relied on a stranger who could have left me stranded in the middle of nowhere but just like my driver in Georgia he was trustworthy and friendly. Over the course of so many years of visiting countries in Eastern Europe I have become a bit of a fan of countries with very little tourism and I almost prefer that over the 'usual' city breaks. It is fair to say that I would probably choose Kiev over Paris or Skopje over Brussels, for instance.

One of the most fascinating countries to visit within the UEFA members list is certainly Israel. It is obviously a place with stricter border control and safety precautions. Over the years, I was lucky that a number of my friends had been either studying or working in countries where I was keen on seeing football. Argentina, the United States, Spain or Israel, I always used the opportunity to visit friends when possible. What impressed me about Israel is the difference in lifestyle between Tel Aviv and Jerusalem. Tel Aviv is an extremely modern city where people are in incredible physical shape and active on the beaches—which is related to mandatory service in the army. In contrast, having a few beers in the ancient port city of Jaffa, is very popular amongst locals and tourists and the nightlife is well known.

Jerusalem on the other side is the city of religions as it is divided in a Jewish, Christian and Muslim part. It is incredibly interesting although I felt a bit of tension being surrounded due to the overwhelming meaning of religion in that area and also a bit out of place at the stunning Western Wall. Out of place in the sense that I was a tourist looking at others praying. I noticed a kid probably aged around twelve who was praying so strongly and convincingly, which I will never forget. Next to the Western Wall is a synagogue which is accessible to everyone and once again, I felt a bit out of place not wanting to disturb the praying Jewish community. It was a fascinating sight but probably just a once in a lifetime experience. Football—which is rare on my travels—was not the main reason for my trip to Israel because there was so much to see, but I was obviously happy that I attended a Maccabi Tel Aviv home match at Bloomfield Stadium (prior to its renovation) to add Israel to my UEFA list. When leaving Israel there are quite a number of random questions to be asked by the homeland security which was fairly interesting. I mentioned to the security police that one reason for my trip was to see the Bloomfield Stadium which raised some further questions as the ground is nothing special and even more bizarre from the border security's point of view was why a football fan from Germany wanted to visit the fixture Maccabi Tel Aviv v Hapoel Be'er Sheva... I managed to explain it and after I cleared up two more dubious requests, I was able to proceed to the gate. The first added question by the police officer was what 'AFA' stands for on my bag. It was a bag from the Argentinian Football Association I was carrying with me and secondly, I was asked about the match I attended and I said: 'It was not great, Maccabi won 5–0'. The reply was: 'Not great and 5–0!?!' I obviously meant it in the sense that the opponent was so poor that it was a low quality game, but the guy eventually realized that I am just a football nutter and he let me pass without too much hassle. It is one of these random stories only groundhoppers experience and not many people outside the football world really understand.

And then there are those venues that simply make very little sense. The most controversial topic is surely Qatar to host the next World Cup but there is one final that comes to my mind as being a very odd event. The Europa League final 2019 in Azerbaijan between Arsenal and Chelsea was certainly a fixture that represented the downside of modern football. Baku as a city is actually a pretty interesting place with its location on the Caspian Sea, several UNESCO heritage sights and a bit of wealth as well. It used to be part of the Soviet Union which is visible outside the main tourist areas and I was struggling a bit to see it as part of Europe really although Azerbaijan is a member of the UEFA. It is at least questionable that it had been chosen as the final venue of such competition and the tipping of the iceberg was that two London teams met each other in Baku. It is bizarre that two clubs from the same league and city were to fly over five hours for a European final to a place that is hardly located in Europe. In the end, it turned out to be a match with extremely limited support by each fan base, a lot of locals and empty seats and a final that felt like a pre-season warm-up game. The Olympic Stadium in Baku is a ground that does not fail to impress with its lit-up outside construction and some big stands. However, the stands are way too far away from the pitch and it is difficult to create any type of atmosphere. I think the Europa League final 2019 will always be remembered as a match that nobody cared too much about. A match between two London sides in a city very far away in a competition valued way below the Champions League is not something football fans usually look forward to. Chelsea won 4–1 comfortably on a night that allowed me to tick Azerbaijan off my list. I also recall several Eintracht Frankfurt supporters in Baku who were beaten on penalties in the semi-final by Chelsea and a fan base that seemed to be keen on the Europa League like no other. Every round, Frankfurt sold-out their home stadium with stunning choreographies and travelled in big numbers to away games. Obviously, Frankfurt's supporters gambled and booked flights early to Baku but it is a great effort to still make the trip far east for a final with their own team ultimately not being involved in.

I get asked regularly about the most scenic stadiums I have seen in Europe and there are plenty to name. Coming from the Hamburg area originally I always had a bit of a connection to

Scandinavia because my first holidays as a kid were frequent journeys to Denmark with its quiet and windy beaches. Renting a holiday house somewhere near Vejle, Kolding or Esbjerg are my oldest memories of travelling abroad. I love Scandinavia in the summer and the city of Bergen in Norway with its houses on various hills is surely one of the nicest places I have ever been. Brann Bergen's stadium itself might not be the most stunning one as it is a fairly average arena but the surrounding areas are particularly beautiful. Football grounds located in the mountains are also venues that always impress me. The Alps offer great opportunities for lovely landscape and the Rheinparkstadion in Vaduz (Liechtenstein) has become a bit of a must see ground for football fans due to mountain ranges being very close. I also was lucky enough to attend a Champions League qualifier in Andorra right in the midst of the Euro 2016 in France. From our location in Carcassonne, a beautiful town in southern France, my wife and I drove up the Pyrenees to see this tiny country in between Spain and France. The journey up to Andorra la Vella is an adventure itself and requires a bit of driving skills and in the summer, it offers some stunning views—although, Andorra is more a skiing haven. The Estadi Comunal d'Andorra Vella is a tiny ground with a capacity of just 1,300 and the mountains in the background are overwhelmingly huge compared to the stadium. Needless to say that the scenic view was more of an attraction than the fixture between FC Santa Coloma and Armenian side Alashkert FC that day.

I usually manage to stay out of dangerous situations especially in countries where people do not speak English but I did gamble once for the sake of ticking off Montenegro's Podgorica City Stadium.

I took advantage of yet another destination with a direct

flight from London which obviously helped significantly on my quest of European football travelling. This time it was Montenegro on my list and the first bad news came before even jumping on the plane as the mid-week fixture of Buducnost Podgorica was decided to take place behind closed doors after some crowd trouble. I was fortunate enough to know a journalist in Belgrade who had helped me attend the Serbian Cup final 2015 at the legendary Rajko Mitić Stadium—Serbia's Marakana. It gave me the chance to get hold of a press pass for the game in Podgorica. It is not great to see a match without fans but my main priority was to tick off Montenegro so I was happy enough to get access to the stadium. The problem for me started at half-time. Due to the fact that there were no fans allowed, no beverages and snacks were available either accordingly so I decided to leave the press area at half-time in order to buy something at the café adjacent to the stadium. Unfortunately, someone decided to lock the door at half-time so my access back to the stand for the second half was denied. Even a guy sitting at the café who recommended knocking on the door strongly could not prevent me from choosing a different solution of following the second 45 minutes of this low quality fixture. In the first half I already noticed a group of roughly 50 Buducnost Ultras who were following the match from a house behind the stadium. It was a house that had never been finished and was basically a ruin—nothing unusual in former Yugoslavia, an area hit hard by the Balkan War in the 90's. Needless to say, it was a very risky idea to meet these Ultras, and to follow the game from up high which could have caused problems. Not only were there a lot of obstacles getting up there, the main danger were these die-hard fans who certainly do not welcome everyone in their group especially without speaking the Montenegrin language. I managed to get up there and the capo straight away asked me who I was. Fortunately, he spoke English and I was able to explain the situation to him and even better was the fact that Montenegro was one of the last destinations on the Balkan for me so I was able to talk about football grounds in former Yugoslavia with him as I had a bit of knowledge on it. We talked about Hajduk Split, FK Sarajevo and the desire of the Buducnost Ultras to play a Serbian side at some point in the Europa League due to the big rivalry for Montenegrins when it comes to Serbia. In this manner I was at least able to follow the rest of the game to some degree although I was a bit busy talking to the capo and I had to keep my eyes open. They could have easily thrown me from this ruin which would have been my end and also, the police could have shown up at any point to end this forbidden assembly. I would have struggled to explain myself without speaking Montenegrin and in hindsight I was very lucky that day—something I would not do again...I guess...groundhoppers are willing to do a lot to tick off a ground on their list, even if it is just a 48-hour bus ride or sleeping at an airport for several days.

The local dish, Cevapcici, I ordered post-match in downtown Podgorica tasted like victory because I managed to get everything done safely. I can't do revisits too often because of my extensive list of new grounds, however, some cities I have seen numerous times and I have a feeling I will return to Montenegro again to attend a more stress-free fixture with fans allowed next time.

The experience in Podgorica also made me think about the difference between countries on the UEFA map in terms of difficulty level. Eastern Europe can be a bit unpredictable at times due to late changes of fixtures and kick-off times, lack of infrastructure or communicational issues. I have to say though that in most cases it had been pretty straight-forward and travelling in Europe regardless of the country is usually very easy. So Africa, South America or Asia can sometimes be more of an adventure which is a great incentive as well. I am not seeking tricky situations but ticking off a ground with a bit of a difficulty level involved makes it surely a bit special.

Scandinavia is certainly an area where groundhopping is extremely easy. It all runs like a clockwork, none of the countries are highly populated so it is all very easy going and everyone speaks perfect Oxford English. Places like Iceland or the Faroe Islands are amongst the friendliest people I have ever met in Europe which is partly a mentality thing but also the enjoyment of the locals to speak to foreigners. I think it is connected to a low populated community who are not 'fed up' with people in overcrowded cities like London, Paris or Berlin. I fully enjoyed the few days I spent in Reykjavík, the capital of Iceland, a very small football nation who at the time just started to become seriously competitive in world football as they later on managed to make the Euro 2016 quarter-finals and the World Cup 2018 which is quite remarkable for a nation of just over 360,000 people. I still have to smile when I remember attending Iceland's U21 qualifier v Kazakhstan in Kópavogur as the players were hardly able to kick a corner due to the strong winds. It was a bit of a ninety minute struggle but the quest of a new country off the bucket list made it an inevitable match to attend and I was fortunate to see another game that day which saw Iceland's seniors beat Albania 2–1 in Reykjavík. For stadium hoppers attending two or even three matches in one day is pretty much as good as it gets and in Iceland it was one of those days.

Another very scenic setting is Gibraltar. The Victoria Stadium is a small ground located right next to the runway of

Gibraltar's airport so one can see plenty of planes landing and departing which is quite impressive especially because the planes look huge in comparison to the football pitch. Even more beautiful is the Rock of Gibraltar which is in very close range to the ground and a nudge more interesting than the two leagues games on amateur level I attended over there. Tickets for the Gibraltar National League are free of charge so basically you just walk through the turnstiles to the ground and it has a cosy bar inside. It is an easy ground to tick off. Obviously, the city centre, Gibraltar Airport and the Spanish border are all within walking distance so it is all straight forward in theory. Unfortunately, the airport has one of the most difficult landing strips which I experienced very closely. My plane coming from London was not able to land in order to return to Gatwick so a shuttle bus to Málaga Airport for an alternative departure caused major delays and that sadly resulted in me not being able to attend the Champions League blockbuster Arsenal v Bayern Munich the next day as I had a ticket for the match. It is another classic groundhopper story that I sacrificed a Champions League match for a double header in the Gibraltar First Division.

It is inevitable that the quest of attending a match in every European country includes very dull football fixtures so flying three or four hours for a low quality game is something I have experienced quite often. I attended a cup semi-final in Moldova between Hîncești and Tiraspol just outside the capital Chișinău which was a pretty brutal level of play. The town looked like a very classic former Soviet location with one of these orthodox churches and its golden domes. Once again, I relied on a driver who waited outside the small ground for the return back to Chișinău after the match. Thinking about it I actually hired a driver fairly often in Eastern Europe which just gets me from hotel / hostel to the ground faster and to not rely on (unpredictable) public transport. It is also very cheap compared to other parts of Europe. The driver in Moldova charged me around twenty-five Euros for about four hours as he had to wait the entire match before heading back to the capital. I had to skip extra-time in that cup game because it would have been rather tricky to be stuck in that town if the driver had left after ninety minutes. What I also remember are the supporters of Sheriff Tiraspol which is quite a big club in Moldova and them showing up with a few Ultras. Tiraspol is the largest city of the Transnistria region which is an unofficial breakaway state with closer ties to the former Soviet Union than to Moldova itself. Russian and Ukrainian are official languages in Transnistria and make up over fifty percent of the population. That explained a decent amount of police forces at the game and an atmosphere that really reminded me of Europe in the 80's.

I had a similar experience near Pristina in Kosovo. A country that had only gained independence in 2008 following the Kosovo War obviously has a very different setting from other European countries in the west, but my journeys to former Yugoslav countries have always been a pleasure so I was impressed how the locals handled their situation including a very welcoming attitude. It was quite remarkable to hear the English and German language skills of most people I have spoken to. Due to the fact that FC Pristina was in the process of refurbishing their stadium the league match I was about to attend had been moved to a small ground in Drenas about thirty minutes from Pristina. The ground did have a stand and a roof but it had never been fully finished so it was basically a construction site. On top of that there was no public toilet so I had to use the restroom of the away team which was fortunately provided by one of the security guards who kind of understood what I wanted without him speaking English. The faces of the coach and players I will never forget when they saw me coming in the middle of their pre-match speech. It underlines though how helpful the people are especially when you consider that they get paid very little. I have heard people asking me: 'Why are you going to Kosovo or Moldova?' Of course, it is part of a special quest otherwise I would have never travelled to these places but in most cases, it was extremely enjoyable and made me think outside the box.

In contrast, I have also seen a few unpleasant scenes such as the qualifier Bulgaria v Croatia in Sofia which had to be abandoned for a short spell due to crowd trouble. It was one of those fixtures with a decent amount of troublemakers which from a football point of view is never great. I started loving this game from the early days so I never understood using sport as a platform for trouble and violence but I can see the trigger game days provide for some. In a country like Bulgaria, for instance, prospects for young people are quite grim and the possibilities are very limited including a ruthless police force so these kinds of fixtures are options to let off a bit of steam. And obviously this kind of frustration level one occasionally observes in struggling countries. I remember that in Albania waiters were not too keen on serving a football tourist like me simply because of them being underpaid and there might be a bit of jealousy involved that I was able to sit outside with my beer while others had to work. Customer service certainly does not apply to all places and I have seen a few times that it was more a waiter versus guest scenario which was rare though but it happens and I take it with a sense of humour. It also depends on where you are. In some places in Europe it is not the best idea to speak English or be considered British, in other areas it is not recommended to try your luck with

'Do you speak German?' which is a topic I will tackle later on.

Football travellers usually try to see as many new grounds as possible when visiting a respective country. In an ideal world, two or three matches a day is a perfect scenario which includes a 'main game' or 'must see stadium' and then one or two smaller grounds in the area that allows one to tick off more venues in one day or consecutive days. To my surprise, I have not found any day in my personal statistics that I ever attended three matches in one day. Stats are very important for groundhoppers to archive the fixtures, the score, attendance and optionally the ticket price. I did see up to four grounds in four consecutive days and attended two matches in one day on plenty of occasions. Very popular for instance is a senior national team fixture in the evening and the U21's or U19's youth national team playing nearby in the afternoon. I did that in Iceland with the mentioned trip to the Reykjavík area, in Wales where I was able to see Wales U21's at Stebonheath Park in Llanelli and then later that day Wales seniors facing Austria in an international qualifier in Swansea and also for the U21 Euros in Denmark with an earlier kick-off in Viborg and then an evening game in Midtjylland. The same is possible for European Cups or certain league games. There are either two grounds in nearby cities such as my trip to Schalke 04 U19's who played their youth game in Erkenschwick not far from Gelsenkirchen and then later I attended the Champions League tie Schalke v Sporting Lisbon. Even easier was the double header in Leverkusen as their U19's ground is right next to the BayArena which is ideal for an afternoon kick-off, a few beers in between and then an 8.45pm kick-off in the Champions League. What I remember mostly from Leverkusen's U19 was not the match itself but plenty of jobless managers who showed up 'for networking purposes' including loads of agents. One of them was

Mike Büskens who managed Greuther Fürth when they got promoted to the Bundesliga and who is widely known in Germany for being part of the Schalke squad that won the UEFA-Cup in 1997. Most recently, I remember doing a so-called 'double header' to revisit Old Trafford and then later that Saturday in January 2019 to see Stockport County for the first time which was a short Uber ride between the grounds.

Attending football matches on consecutive days is also very popular and a bit of common sense for major tournaments such as the Euros or the World Cup. Similar here, a groundhopper picks the stadium or fixture that is priority and builds a few more fixtures around it. 2012 was one of my most successful years as I was able to attend seventy fixtures. It included five games within eight days seeing Villa Park, St James Park, St Andrews Stadium, The Hawthorns and Bramall Lane in a short period of time. Another highlight was seeing St. Pauli at Hertha Berlin on a Monday, Benfica against Celtic on a Tuesday in the Champions League followed by another Champions League tie on Wednesday in Porto which involved Dinamo Zagreb being the visitors. The reason I mention Zagreb in particular is that I visited a football store in Lisbon prior to the game in Porto with scarves available from various clubs. Randomly, they had a Hajduk Split scarf who are Dinamo's arch rivals. I bought the scarf due to the fact that I did not have the time when I visited Split's Poljud Stadium in 2010 for my collection. Obviously, I did not think about it when I opened my backpack at Porto Airport at the security control surrounded by Dinamo fans who were on the way home as well. Luckily, I noticed my mistake straight away to avoid an unnecessary brawl. In fact, in some cities or clubs with a strong, die-hard fan base, groundhoppers are not that welcome anymore almost in the sense that random fans are entering a forbidden territory. I have not experienced it personally but I have seen pictures on the way to a football ground with graffiti saying 'groundhopper go home!' There is a bit of truth to it because stadium hoppers do not necessarily contribute to the atmosphere nor do they care too much about the result of the match. This is fundamentally different from supporting your own club week in and week out. The main reason for me to pursue ticking off stadiums is probably the fact that the club I support will never play in Europe—unless St. Pauli unexpectedly win the German Cup which is extremely unlikely to ever happen. Basically, the only time I can see new stadiums is when my team gets promoted or relegated which really makes it difficult to work on an extended list of venues. A team that regularly plays in the Champions League or Europa League gives much more opportunities to travel within Europe and for fans to support their own club at the same time. That also explains the fact that a lot of supporters of the English national team are from lower league clubs who will never play in European competitions.

What I have also been doing more in recent years are football day trips. This is connected to two factors: a) I am a family man now having less time and b) London is a great place to fly out and return on the same day because it has so many flight options. One of the first times I did this was seeing AS Roma playing at the iconic Olympic Stadium. It included flying out early in the morning, a quick trip to the Vatican and the Colosseum and then an on-time arrival at the ground which is highly recommended because AS Roma have one of the best pre-match anthems in football in my opinion. Over the years, I have done these kinds of day trips quite extensively such as Málaga on a beautiful Sunday in January, Zlatan Ibrahimovic's home club Malmö FF with very close proximity to Copenhagen Airport and Lublin in Poland for the U20's World Cup. Sleeping at airports is an option as well but it is a more tiring option the older I get. I do remember doing it on several occasions though in Paris, Geneva, Hannover, Bucharest, Vilnius and Madrid. The latter destination was a bit odd due to a disc jockey who seemingly spent several days at Barajas Airport. It was one of those trips where I only spent about twelve hours in town just to see Rayo Vallecano in Madrid. Upon arrival on the way to the public transport I saw this DJ already in the afternoon mixing some tunes on his notebook and then later on again when I returned to the airport to kill about six hours prior to my plane departing back to London. He annoyed a fairly decent amount of people as he was still working on making some music in the middle of the night. Barajas Airport is a major hub to South America so it is always quite busy and everyone was annoyed but it seemed like nobody dared to say anything as the disc-jockey looked extremely stressed (possibly drug influenced). My guess was that he did not sleep at all for days and probably experienced a flight cancellation or even more likely, he missed his flight. I was happy to listen to a Mike McCarthy press conference that night who was just appointed as head coach of the Dallas Cowboys which was interesting enough in the midst of the NFL Playoffs and distracted me from spending the night at an airport.

Chapter 5
Tickets

Groundhoppers have a special desire for collections. Obviously ticking off football stadiums is a bit of an unusual passion due to the difficulty of the task and a certain randomness of fixtures. It is certainly a bit easier to sit at home watching football on the couch rather than flying over five hours to Baku one-way for a ninety minute encounter between two sides I have basically no relation with.

Additionally, it is not only seeing a new stadium but other memorabilia that football fans collect on game day. The match programme can be a collector's item to read a few stories on the respective clubs and especially for fixtures that have a personal value such as a local derby, a game far away or a match with a higher value such as a final. I attended the Champions League final twice in 2011 and 2012 and buying a match programme was mandatory as a souvenir. I was never the most passionate collector of match programmes though. It is pretty clear, for example, that a lot of pre-match programmes by the respective managers are not really written by the coach, but an editor who is involved with the creation of the programme. There are exceptions though and other football fans are in fact keen collectors of these programmes which I experienced once when I attended a football match programmes fair in London. Others collect beer cups from each football ground or buy scarves or jerseys of every club they have seen a home match of. I used to do that as well but it takes away quite a lot of space so ultimately, I stuck with my main collector's item: the match ticket. I mentioned before that I only ever lost a match ticket twice so since being a teenager I have been very keen on collecting the ticket and put it in a special folder to keep them all preserved. I have to admit that I enjoy a new football ground even more if the respective club prints nice looking tickets. I am certainly not a fan of 'print-at-home' or tickets to be downloaded on the smartphone which has become more and more popular these days. The worst for me is no ticket at all which I can understand for lower league clubs due to the financial aspect of printing a paper match ticket but I do remember several occasions where it was a bit of a downer that there were no tickets available when paying at the gate. The fifty-five UEFA members are a huge personal target and I would have loved to have a match ticket for every country. In Gibraltar, for instance, it is free entry so I just walked through to the ground on match day which means I have no ticket as 'evidence' from the two league matches I attended. I make about twenty to thirty pictures from every game but the match ticket for me was always the main item to collect. It is that important to me that I am aiming to return to Gibraltar at some point to get a match ticket. If a team plays in European competitions, they have to print match tickets or if Gibraltar builds their new stadium in the not so distant future I am likely to return to the British Overseas Territory to get that important collector's item. Even trickier is Moldova for me. When I booked my flights to Chișinău from Luton—an airport ideal for travelling to Eastern Europe—I gambled because I did not know at the time who would be playing the cup semi-finals. I was pretty sure that out of the four teams at least one of them would be playing in the Chișinău area and my hope was FC Zimbru as their ground is located pretty centrally in the capital, a stadium I ended up passing by on the way from the airport to the city centre. Unfortunately, Zimbru were drawn away to Bălți, a city two hours by car from Chișinău. The second semi-final was played between FC Petrocub against Sheriff Tiraspol, a fixture I had mentioned earlier. I did talk to someone prior to my journey who had watched a game in Bălți before and he said that they hand out paper match tickets at the turnstiles. My next gamble was now whether I should travel the minimum two hours to Bălți to ensure the match ticket or to prefer Petrocub just outside of Chișinău for a shorter way of travel. I contacted someone at Petrocub ahead of the fixture, but they struggled to understand what I really wanted so I decided in the end to choose the ground closer to my location regardless that my request did not find an answer. Unfortunately for me, it was free entry and no paper match ticket which surely made me the only person at this small ground to be upset that fans did not have to pay for entry in order to get my beloved collector's item.

I once bought a ticket on match day in Madrid at Rayo Vallecano despite the fact that I was offered to attend the match for free because next to the turnstile a season ticket holder had a spare season ticket from his friend who could not make the Wednesday night clash against Lugo in the Segunda División. I tried to explain to him in broken Spanish that I collect match tickets so I would need to buy a ticket rather than getting in for free and then return the season ticket after the match. Another man heard the conversation and translated in broken English to me that this is an offer I should not refuse because once again, I could go for free. Both eventually left very irritated after I explained it again and bought my ticket for fifteen Euros—an amount I was very happy to pay due to the mentioned passion for collecting match tickets. I know it is tough to understand for some, but with all the efforts involved in travelling to these various grounds it really is a bit of a trophy to bring a paper match ticket home and put it in my ticket stub folder. These tickets have very little value to others but are personally very important so if anyone ever breaks into my apartment I would prefer losing my television or smartphone rather than my football ticket collection. Spain is a special scenario anyway because the quality of the ink on the tickets is pretty much the worst of all tickets I have been collecting world-wide. My first ever Spanish ground was Real Madrid in 2004 at the legendary Bernabéu and the ink of the ticket has faded completely. The same happened to Atlético Madrid, FC Sevilla, Real Mallorca and once again Real Madrid when I attended the Bernabéu for a second time in 2017 in the Champions League against Tottenham. I am still hopeful that the match tickets I possess for FC Barcelona, Villarreal, Valencia and several other Spanish football clubs keep the ink to some degree but the paper they have been using for the match tickets does not seem to be ideal at all to keep it preserved for a longer period of time. On top of that, I had a special experience in Bilbao where I could not obtain a match ticket. The Estadio San Mamés was under construction at the time including one stand missing so I was not aware that only season ticket holders and members were allowed to gain entrance for their La Liga match against Celta Vigo. As far as I remember there is a university faculty opposite the football ground so I was able to ask a few students regarding the chances of obtaining a match ticket. Fortunately, someone was able to help me borrow a season ticket on the day just for the match. I had to pay a bit of extra money for it but I was happy to do that and even more so when I met the person who had the spare season ticket. It was an elderly man at least in his 70's who did not speak English but due to my conversational level of Spanish language skills we were able to talk a bit. Basically, he had to hand me the season ticket at the stadium entrance and then I would return the ticket to him straight after we passed the turnstiles. Due to the fact that I met him roughly ninety minutes before kick-off we had to kill some time and he basically reinvested the money straight away into a box of cigarillos and some beers. It was an odd but not unpleasant situation to spend one and a half hours with a stranger in a 'cervecería' in Bilbao considering the language barrier and the fact that I was not even an Athletic supporter in the first place. However, football is a language itself and it was certainly not the first time I would speak with someone about sports without meeting the same language skills. It meant that I would be able to take Bilbao's home ground off my list, but unfortunately I was not able to keep a match ticket for my collection. I did make a picture of that season ticket with my phone though to at least have some memorabilia.

Bilbao is part of the Basque region which is quite fascinating as large parts of their population seek independence from Spain and the area suffered immensely under the Franco regime so the supporters have quite a rebellious attitude which makes it a very interesting place to go. I certainly would not mind coming back to the city and watching another game to finally get my Athletic match ticket but as mentioned before, the poor quality of Spanish paper match tickets will probably make the ink to fade within a few months anyway…

I obtained a number of tickets throughout the years that really were a disappointment. Usually, when ticket providers and ticket sales companies make the ticket is much worse than tickets originally printed by the respective clubs. Ticket sales companies print the same format for all the clubs that use this kind of service in comparison to clubs that put a bit of thought into the ticket layout. Generally speaking, traditional clubs design some really decent tickets especially when their heyday was a while ago to hark back to the 'good old days'. German teams like Eintracht Braunschweig, 1. FC Kaiserslautern or Alemannia Aachen who are now playing in lower leagues are one of those traditional teams to name who really emphasise on their history and that includes their tickets. In Great Britain it is pretty similar and it probably goes down deeper to non-league clubs than in other European countries as a lot of British clubs were founded a long time ago being the motherland of association football. St Albans City, for instance, a club that plays in the National League South currently (sixth tier in the English football pyramid) have one of the nicest tickets I have ever bought. My all-time favourite is probably RC Lens who printed a feature of what looks to be the French Revolution on their ticket, I think in terms of style it could not be made any better than that. Another lovely design is the press pass I was able to obtain for the cup final in Serbia because it is printed on a proper plastic surface and logos of both teams involved. I think that's how a ticket should look like for a final on neutral ground.

As mentioned, no ticket at all is the worst for a ticket collector but some printouts were specifically poor such as Brøndby IF in Denmark or KF Teuta in Albania who looked like supermarket receipts. I was unlucky in Northern Ireland as I attended two cup games at the Oval at Glentoran and Solitude in Belfast respectively—two very traditional British football grounds with a lot of history and a bit of a 'breeze from the past'.

It turned out that there were no paper match tickets printed for those cup ties, probably due to financial reasons, so I just paid at the gate and walked through without a ticket which seemingly was not the case for the 'normal' league matches. More and more stewards outside stadiums in Britain have realized that though, because a few times when I asked if I can buy a ticket at the gate the reply was: 'You can buy at the gate, but they haven't got paper tickets so if you collect tickets buy them at the fan shop or ticket office.' It is pretty much evidence that collecting match tickets is popular amongst football fans. I certainly aim to frame several hundred football tickets from Germany, England, Scotland, the UEFA members and a number of FIFA countries at some point as soon as I obtain them from all the traditional clubs and countries that are on my 'to-do-list'. It is getting tougher nowadays though because 'print-at-home'-tickets and downloads on mobile phones seem to be the future so just like the traditional football stadiums with its iconic floodlights paper match tickets are soon to die out sadly.

Chapter 6
What makes a great stadium?

When visiting different stadiums almost on a weekly basis one develops something like a 'groundhopper instinct'. Ten or fifteen years ago when it was not that easy to find football grounds via apps or maps on the smartphone I needed a certain instinct to find a ground. Usually, I would arrive at a train station in an unfamiliar city or foreign country and needed to navigate my way to find the respective stadium. What is more and more gone are floodlights that are great markers to find what I am looking for. New arenas don't have the classic floodlights anymore which is a shame for nostalgic football fans and I agree that it was a very important feature in order to find the ground and also to appreciate the surroundings of a stadium. I personally think that the outside view of a stadium and its location are pretty vital factors for football fans to enjoy the matchday experience. I still grew up in a time where floodlights were a normal feature of football stadiums and I am pleased to have actively lived through that time. Those pictures when hundreds of supporters were making their way to the ground on a rainy cold night with huge floodlights in sight are still very fresh in mind as a young football fan. Braunschweig, Bochum, Dresden or the Niedersachsenstadion in Hannover were my first memories of these kind of images on match days when growing up as a football fan in Germany and to this day I worship these experiences because stadiums nowadays look very different and many arenas are a bit boring. It is still possible to attend 'old school' football grounds in lower tiers or in other parts of the world such as Eastern Europe or South America but even over there newly built stadiums are very common and have replaced historic football grounds. One of the more recent memories that really represent the old 'Eastern bloc' venues with its large parades under communist reign back then was my visit to the Stadium Pasienky in Bratislava in 2011. In terms of capacity it is actually nowhere near the big stadiums in Moscow, Kiev or Leipzig (back then in the Soviet Union and GDR respectively) but these huge floodlights I always remember as the main feature on a rainy summer day in the Slovakian capital for a rather uninspiring meeting with Andorra in a Euro qualifier. The day before I had visited Austria against Germany at the Ernst-Happel-Stadion in Vienna which is one of those big ovals that were the norm for a national stadium from a few decades ago. All these football grounds are getting replaced by multi-functional arenas now and sometimes not even paying cash is possible anymore but with a so-called club card.

Location is also key for me in order to like a stadium. I am fortunate enough to support a football club that is located right in the heart of Hamburg and its nightlife district. On matchday it creates a certain vibe that is connected to the respective fan scenes. The bars and stadium pubs around the Millerntorstadium are distinctive and strongly connected to FC St. Pauli. This to me makes a traditional football club and its surroundings. If you were to make a picture of a street, a local bar or a landmark near a football ground without the stadium actually being in that picture and you can still more or less figure out which football club it is that to me makes a great sight of a football ground. If a stadium is located in the middle of nowhere such as the Allianz-Arena in Munich or a new stadium is located quite far from its origin, it takes away a bit of a soul that every club has got. For example, I never really got over the fact that West Ham United left Upton Park and moved to the Olympic Stadium for profit reasons. Upton Park represented this special east London working class vibes which was unique for that area. As soon as you got out of Plaistow or West Ham tube station I realized: 'Clearly, this is West Ham United'. It doesn't really matter if you like the club or not or if you don't care about them, but Upton Park and the filthy pubs around, the fish and chip shops and the cockney accent sounding all over the place were distinctive and representative of the football club. A great example of how a club should represent itself, its values and imply its origin. West Ham to me stands for working class and you can't try to 'upgrade' things by artificially making them look more 'posh' to attract a different type of fan base or even tourists. I visited Upton Park three times and, although I did not cheer for any team on the three occasions, I always fully enjoyed being there because it was authentic. Since West Ham moved to Olympic Stadium I was there once to see football for one simple reason: to tick the ground off. It is a stadium located next to Stratford Shopping Centre with the stands being far from the pitch—as it hosted the 2012 Summer Olympics and a needed running-track—and a fairly horizontal stand which takes away a decent amount of noise coming from the supporters.

Since the early days I have been a fan of vertical stands. I think I first realized that at the European Championships in 2000 at the Stade de Sclessin in Liége (Belgium), a stadium with three tier vertical stands and a very loyal fan base which I found out on my second visit to see local side Standard rather than two national teams playing at the Euros. On top of that, I think keeping as many terraces as possible is an important atmosphere booster. In many cases, terraces are located behind the goal nowadays, the most famous probably being the impressive 'Yellow Wall' at the Westfalenstadion in Dortmund. I do like terraces that ideally surround the stadium in three or even four sections. It is very difficult to put in place these days especially when considering UEFA regulations but at least to some degree it is still possible. A famous stadium refurbishment in recent years has been Union Berlin, a football club and stadium located in Köpenick, an area in East Berlin quite far away from all the tourism and famous sights of the German capital. Union Berlin and the Köpenick area are pretty much what West Ham and Upton Park were for East London or Highbury for Arsenal, something indispensable connected to each other. The only difference is that Union Berlin managed to enhance the meaning of its stadium and to keep its history alive. The supporters themselves helped to build new stands and it is now a football ground with seventy-five percent terraces, very rare for a member of a major European football league. Connected to that, it is inevitable to mention the value of ticket prices. It makes a huge difference to keep affordable prices at least for the terraces to allow fans from every social class to be in the position to purchase tickets. In most cases the die-hard fan bases are not a very wealthy group of people. This trend has certainly destroyed the atmosphere in the English Premier League and has caused the interesting development that a number of British football fans have adopted their German team to support a club 'from the old days': affordable ticket prices, terraces and alcohol to be consumed inside the stadium. It has even gotten to the degree that

English fan clubs have been formed for German fourth tier clubs such as Alemannia Aachen.

The stadium experience for a groundhopper is very different for someone who is attending a football match to see his/her team play. As a supporter more or less only the result counts. Of course, you meet friends, you socialise and talk about non-football related matters, you enjoy the atmosphere and togetherness but when your club is playing the mood for the rest of the weekend relies on the result of your beloved team. For a groundhopper a lot of things that happen around the events on the pitch are equally important if not more than that. The pictures you take, the design of the match ticket, the behaviour and chants of the Ultras, the quality of the food and the beers, all these factors are something to remember and to rate as a stadium traveller. There are certainly fixtures where the match itself is not interesting at all and I have made that experience on several occasions. One venue I always mention is the Moses Mabhida Stadium in Durban which is one of my favourite constructions. It has a beautiful white roof with a bow and it is beautifully located near the beach. When I attended South Africa's African Cup of Nations group game against Morocco in 2013 I was hoping for the hosts to win because everyone around me supported the Bafana Bafana so I naturally went for the home team to win. But to be honest, it did not really make a difference personally who would win this match. Some people—even if it is two neutral teams—they have to cheer for someone. I do recall attending the World Cup 2006 match Argentina against Ivory Coast in Hamburg where a German guy in front of me was wearing an Ivory Coast jersey. Basically, on that evening this fan became a supporter of Didier Drogba and his teammates for ninety minutes. Over the course of the match he got extremely passionate about the game that he looked seriously hurt emotionally when Ivory Coast eventually lost to Argentina two goals to one. This is something I could not even fake. I do have teams I support in different sports but in football I really do have that one team that makes me euphoric when we win and frustrated when we lose—I can't really project that to any other team and I know that St. Pauli are a second-tier club with average results at best usually so the saying 'you don't choose your club, the club chooses you' makes sense in my case. It would certainly be easier to support Real Madrid, Bayern Munich or Liverpool as they simply win much more games per season. So I do not have a problem at all to attend a match without actually picking sides and the day in Durban was a classic example. It was more about experiencing my first football match in Africa and more importantly, to enjoy a stadium with a great architecture. I do not remember much of the game, I know the score was 2–2, but what I recall to this day was looking at all different angles of this football ground and that lovely roof construction. This is evident of how different the stadium experience can be for a groundhopper compared to the regular football fan with his season ticket. I can attend a boring 0–0 somewhere in Belgium's second tier and still have a great evening due to various reasons: I made a nice picture, the beer was exceptionally tasty or simply because the ground was on my list for quite some time. That is actually why a lot of die-hard football fans do not understand the concept of groundhopping. The idea of watching a match without supporting any of the teams is something not everyone understands but it is simply a different angle how ground hunters experience a football day. This aspect leads to another important part of a stadium experience: the people you meet.

Football fans come from various social groups from all parts of society with different opinions and values. In most cases it is great to broaden your horizon and it is simply an important part of travelling. Of course, some football fans and regular travellers do not understand the purpose of a stadium hopper. I think it is fair to say when I tell people about my quest I get everything from fascination and admiration to disbelief. Certainly, some people think it is crazy or weird and some simply do not understand it. In 2013, I attended the FIFA Club World Cup in Morocco where Bayern Munich happened to participate—a fact I could not have cared less about—but I was obviously able to communicate with the Bayern supporters as we spoke the same language—unless a few had a strong Bavarian accent which makes it a bit more difficult. Bayern that evening played Chinese side Guangzhou Evergrande in Agadir and after the match the majority of German supporters enjoyed the obligatory beers in the same hotel that I checked-in. I had a quick chat with a Bayern supporter at the bar who I would say was in his 50's and he only talked about Bayern Munich assuming that I supported the club as well. After I told him that a) I only flew to Morocco to tick off two new football grounds and b) I actually support Bundesliga 2 side St. Pauli he looked at me like I was an alien from a different planet. He just could not understand that I flew all the way to see random football grounds and even more unbelievable for him that I did not support the mighty Bayern. Some fans of bigger clubs do not understand to support the local team from where you are from regardless of the league they play in.

Over the years, I actually reduced the level of info to not further confuse football fans who do not have a connection to groundhopping. For example, I am more and more becoming a guest in my home country Germany because I have been living abroad for roughly ten years now. It means I would fly over from

London to see a football match—possibly a lower league fixture—stay overnight and return to the UK. When I talk to German locals at amateur games and tell them that I flew over from London it is hard for them to comprehend.

Meeting different people on my travels is particularly interesting because there are so many stories involved. The reference point is always travelling as the main topic but the purpose of the journey is different from traveller to traveller. I remember being on a night train from Bergen to Oslo whilst sitting next to an American who wanted to see the beautiful Norwegian fjords and a few other European locations on his list. Without recalling the conversation in detail it was probably one of those once in a lifetime journeys for him to see most of Europe in a matter of three or four weeks. It certainly was a more common purpose of travel than the one I had as I just watched a Brann Bergen home match in the cup the evening before and I was just on my way to the Norwegian capital to see Stabæk IF just outside Oslo. The priorities of traveling are quite an interesting part of it because so many times I met people with different targets on what they would like to see. In Rome you see thousands and thousands of people spending days to see the Vatican, I just queued up, made a few pictures—the same for the Colosseum—and then made my way to the Olympic Stadium to see AS Roma which was the main part of the trip and actually took more time than the sightseeing part. It sometimes reaches a degree that if I had been to a city a couple of times before that I completely focus on ticking off a new ground regardless of the fact that I like the respective city. I have done it in Barcelona where I drove directly from the airport to Espanyol's ground and spent the afternoon in the stadium area, watched the match in the evening and flew back to London early the next morning. In

Madrid I attended a Rayo Vallecano home match, checked out a 'cerveceria' post-match and spent the night at the airport to catch the 6am flight home.

It is also nice to help people a little bit with my passion. Usually, in countries where taxi drivers do not earn a whole lot they always appreciate a longer journey for a price that is acceptable for both parties. I did it several times driving from Skopje to Sofia, Pristina to Skopje, Podgorica to Tivat, Chişinău to Hînceşti, Minsk to Borisov or Vilnius to Kaunas. Renting a car is the more reasonable option most of the time but having a driver is very convenient in countries where it is affordable. In Thailand I was spending a week on the beach with my wife and in order to see at least one match in the Bangkok area I negotiated a price with a driver who was happy to have a three hour stopover in the Thanyaburi district to see a home match of Bangkok Glass. I don't remember the exact amount but it was certainly enough to exceed the usual daily earnings of a local driver in Thailand and the guy was enjoying the game as well with some snacks. It was probably one of his best work days ever considering his excellent mood after we negotiated the deal and he was happy to drive us to the resort straight after the game. Especially in poorer countries it is actually nice to contribute a little bit to the economy although, here and there you get ripped off which is calculated in the budget though. It is a valuable lesson to learn for future trips on top.

I obviously can't close this chapter without mentioning my top three stadiums world-wide which is not an easy task because I could easily name fifty or sixty but when it comes to architecture, atmosphere and simply the unique vibes surrounding the area of the football ground I would go with La Bombonera in the Boca district of Buenos Aires, Celtic Park in

Glasgow and the Moses Mabhida Stadium in Durban.

A big booster of my passion about stadium hunting is the unknown before seeing the terraces for the first time. Those steps up the stands after I bought my ticket are always special when seeing a new ground. Most of the grounds I have seen before on pictures or television but to physically be there is always great and some stadiums and fan bases are simply special. A unique but different feeling I experience as well when the match is over. A new ground ticked off includes extensive travelling, money spent and time dedicated so it has a special type of satisfaction and a feeling of a piece of work finished when I take another ground off my bucket list. At the end of the day, groundhopping remains a very special type of collecting and the project is never fully finished, as soon as I tick off a ground from my list I usually have a new ground in my mind already. It makes me thrive probably until the rest of my life.

Chapter 7
Poland

I mentioned previously that I have visited countries within the UEFA members list that surprised me positively such as Georgia, Ukraine or the Faroe Islands. Iceland is certainly a country to name that is very unique and inspired me to one day visit Greenland and possibly Alaska. Some countries when solely taking the landscape, are traveller hotspots, and rightly so. Norway, Switzerland, Scotland and beyond Europe Canada and New Zealand are some of my favourite destinations because they really cover my main travel priorities including decent food, friendly people, mountains and excellent infrastructure. I do love the adventure as well but the mentioned countries have a lovely feel of familiarity and diversity to them—also from a football point of view. For example, if you watch a match in Glasgow it has a completely different Scottish vibe than attending a match in Inverness. It is a difference between a rough, working-class place and a quiet, rural location which surely has an influence on the local football team and its fan base.

Sometimes the destination is even more important than the respective football ground. It is rare for groundhoppers but it happens. It can be the case that you just want to tick off a certain country without caring too much which ground it is. I had such occasions in Albania, Montenegro or Moldova where it was all about adding the country to my list of places where I had seen at least one football match. And then there are places that have a historical significance, a must-see sight or a personal connection to visit. One of those countries is Poland. In recent years, I added more Polish cities to my list to watch the obligatory football match, but also to experience the people, the culture and historic relevance. Growing up in the late 80's and 90's in northern Germany I barely found someone who would travel to Poland for tourism or holidays unless you had some Polish background (which is not unusual at all in Germany). Even travelling to former GDR cities was not common because the service was considered backward without being particularly welcoming. It is fair to say that it probably had the stereotype of the former Eastern Bloc that travelling to the Netherlands, Denmark, Austria, France or Italy was simply more common. The first time I visited Poland was in 2010 about seven months before I moved to the United Kingdom from Germany. I attended the fixture Lechia Gdańsk against Wisła Kraków at the old Lechii Stadium. Gdańsk is a seaside city that actually does not differ much from the German cities on the Baltic Sea and, historically, the city has both a significant Polish and German heritage because of its strategically important location. Tourism at the time was probably not fully advanced but I certainly did not notice a whole lot of differences compared to western Europe and stereotypes I could not confirm a single bit either.

In 2012 the European Championships took place in Poland and the Ukraine where I was only based in L'viv and Kiev so I did not experience any of the Polish cities during the major tournament. What I did realize though was that tourism must have been boosted due to the international attention such tournaments generally draw to host nations. Every time I visited

Poland in the last eight years it has been an absolute delight and it has become one of my favourite countries to travel—and this is only from a travellers' point of view and does not include any government developments which I see quite critically in many eastern European countries when it comes to civil rights. However, the people of Poland have impressed me during my visits and things certainly have improved in the service sector. I noticed it when I visited the beautiful city of Wrocław in 2018. The market places in Poland are the main spots to hang out like in so many European cities and with live bands playing, fresh food served everywhere and providing a welcoming atmosphere I think Poland is a country now taking full advantage of its value as a great destination for travel.

The positive experience is also connected to the fact that I paid the city of Lublin a visit in 2019. The town was not really on my list—certainly not from a football ground perspective—but after I had done some research, I thought it would be a good idea to get to know Lublin. The football story of the trip is a short one really, I attended a U-20 World Cup fixture between Japan and South Korea in a stadium that had fairly recently been opened in 2014 and looks pretty much like most of the new arenas but still, a ground I enjoyed seeing. However, what I will never forget is the vibe and pulse of Lublin. It is a city that is home to the Lublin Castle and the Cracow Gate which leads right into the Old Town and fortunately has been preserved despite the city's occupation in the Second World War. The preservation is quite key to the fact that Lublin has a special vibe. A number of buildings and restaurants really give you a hint from the past and the locals worship their customs and cuisine to show and explain to foreigners. It a little bit reminded me of Kutaisi in Georgia, not in terms of the places itself, both countries are very different but in the sense that the locals appreciate you visiting the city because Warsaw, Wrocław and surely Kraków are usually destinations with a higher number of tourists coming to Poland especially in the summer. Lublin has a calmness to it that I could have stayed in the Old Town for many hours to check out three or four different locations and simply to enjoy the peaceful atmosphere. It surely had a lot to do with the fact that one inevitably gets confronted with the Nazi German occupation from 1939 to 1944 at a time when chaos and persecution ruled over the city. Quite an astonishing picture is a photo of two SS guards watching over the Lublin ghetto during the occupation. Obviously, I have seen hundreds if not thousands of pictures of World War II as I started early in German school learning about it as part of the history education program. Footage and pictures in particular give you an invaluable insight of how severe and indescribable the situation must have been living in a country run over by a fascist/national socialist army. It connects many life stories and fates of so many people and I think pictures are one great tool of evidence of that time. It was without question that I left the beautiful Old Town of Lublin on that lovely summer day to spend a few hours at Majdanek Concentration Camp and its State Museum which was one of the rare camps actually located within the city borders of Nazi occupied territories. It was not the first time I had visited a concentration camp as I had gone on school trips to Neuengamme, Buchenwald and Sachsenhausen which were a different type of experience because at such a young age you somehow realize what had happened at the time, but it is even tougher to understand as a young teenager. I decided to go to Majdanek because I wanted to and also as an educational duty because evidence of witnesses, pictures and being physically on site is so much more valuable than anything else.

It is even more life changing than the war museum in Kiev I mentioned earlier with the postcards of soldiers covering an entire exhibition room. When I arrived at Majdanek on a fairly hot mid-week afternoon in June 2019 it was not unexpectedly quiet and apart from a small tour guide group there were not more than four or five others visiting the camp while I was there. It is in fact astonishing that it is not more than a fifteen to twenty minute bus ride from Lublin town centre to Majdanek and it barely feels like being located in a remote area like other German-occupied concentration camps during World War II. There is a museum with footage of survivors and witnesses of the camp, a large Mausoleum, a Memorial, a crematorium (partly reconstructed) and several barracks. Inside these barracks are different exhibition themes dedicated to events at Majdanek and the Holocaust. Two images that I particularly remember are a shrine that represents the 'unknown victims' of Majdanek which is visually very moving as the room is full of light bulbs underlined by music. The other image is a large poster in one of the barracks which shows what appears to be a parade in Lublin organized for SS, German Order Police and Wehrmacht staff. I was always interested in having a closer look at pictures of that time to see how the faces of the perpetrators looked like. It is obviously not possible to characterize or define a Nazi *per se* because when a country turns into a fascist state all parts of society are involved and all layers from intellectuals to people of small means played their part in the system. And still, if I look at the faces of the people celebrating their so-called 'Germanisation' of Lublin in that particular photograph I see members of the Wehrmacht, SS or General Government who in my mind struggled to find their place in life and society before Nazi Germany. This could be financial struggles, educational issues, that they were not good enough for university, for instance, or personal problems such as poor character traits, failure and quite possibly self-loathing. I am pretty sure that a lot of these perpetrators knew that the Nazi movement was based— apart from all the racial fanaticism—on lies. They knew they were not all of a sudden a 'master race' but they could very well live with that lie because they were on the winning end of this racial non-sense. Unfortunately, large numbers of perpetrators never experienced any punishment for their actions in this genocide known as 'Operation Reinhard'.

Two years before Lublin I visited Kraków which to me is one of the most beautiful cities in Europe. The market square is picturesque, full of history and also vibrant; being a very popular tourist destination. One evening in June I was attending the U-21 Euro fixture between Denmark and Italy which would eventually turn out to be a football match I could not have cared less about. My wife and I were only in Kraków for three days so I had to find a day for a visit to Auschwitz concentration camp which is about a 1.5 hours' bus journey from the city centre. I think since I was about eighteen years old and having read a decent amount about Auschwitz in school I have had the plan to go. From Hamburg it is relatively far away and back then there were no direct flights to Kraków so it took me until 2019 and thirty-three years of age to finally make the most important trip of my life to a historically highly significant sight. If I look back at my time in school and history classes and compare it to this day and age a lot has changed. From a personal standpoint I have more knowledge on the topic obviously, there is more understanding, there is a lot of empathy required to understand what happened although, the details will always be shocking and outrageous. There is also a level of unpleasant acceptance needed because we can't change the past. The fact that the Holocaust happened and the way the 'Final Solution' was confirmed at the Wannsee Conference, the planning, the execution and the thoroughness was carried out by Germans. It has its birth in Germany, those were German camps in German-occupied territories. To accept a genocide executed by your own country is not easy for some to acknowledge. I personally, however, find this perception extremely important. Nazi Germany did not invent genocide, antisemitism, concentration camps nor 'Germanisation', all that happened and existed before, but Auschwitz and all the other death camps in the occupied zones and in Germany itself was a genocide never to be seen before. The number of victims in such a short period of time, the deliberate actions to strip off any sense of humanity from the inmates and the unprecedented level of torture is part of German history and has to be acknowledged as such and is always to be remembered.

The day our bus departed to Auschwitz was another sunny summer day in Poland which would have been a gorgeous day in Kraków. The road to the concentration camp is not via a freeway so it takes time and it feels a longer journey than it should considering it is just ninety'ish minutes away. When we arrived in the town of Auschwitz it still felt like a while from there before we finally arrived at the camp. There was a little bit of familiarity because those red brick buildings I had seen in various documentaries and the first thing I recognized was the 'Arbeit macht frei' ('work sets you free') sign at the entrance gate with that 'b' being upside down which to this day is considered an act of defiance by the prisoners who had to affix the slogan to the gate. A replica of that 'b' is represented in a sculpture in Berlin and the slogan is one of many macabre signs that the Nazis put on concentration camps. Expressions such as 'Arbeit macht frei' were no invention by the Nazis and existed before but as they used the German language in a very ambiguous way there are lot of sayings that basically can't be used anymore due to their meaning in the Holocaust.

There are two things that hit you straight away when you arrive at Auschwitz I and Birkenau. The one thing is the sheer size of the camp which is difficult to put in words. The number of barracks, the crematoriums, and the administrative headquarters for the SS and security police combined with the realization that the main camp and the death camp in Birkenau only had one purpose is life changing. The tour takes about two to three hours and even then you can't possibly see everything. Moreover, some of the evidence had been destroyed by the Nazis in 1945 due to the advancing Red Army. Regardless, it is a huge complex and the size of the camp is extremely unique.

The second realization is that I have never been to a place where you feel all the energy taken out of your body the longer you walk around the camp. There are so many different places to see such as the aforementioned administrative headquarters, a hospital (that never was treated as such), several places of medical experiments and other forms of torture, gas chambers, barracks in inhuman conditions, train wagons and countless pictures of human beings murdered including children. At the end of the day when I sat down on the bus I felt like all my energy of this day was gone and obviously, there was a sense of shock. I generally have to say that sorrow is certainly part of all of this, but particularly on this day I felt an incredible amount of anger. Anger against the people who carried all of this out and who thought that this was the right thing to do. I sometimes wish I could talk to one of the perpetrators to see what was going on in their minds because it is impossible for me to understand. There will never be any type of comprehension. Certainly my path of life is a completely different one as I have nothing in common with them apart from the fact that these murderers were born in the same country than I was with the significant difference that their birth year was around 1890–1900 and I was born in 1983 which makes the circumstances of growing-up utterly differential and my views on the world are distinctively contrasting.

I was lucky enough to listen to a Hungarian Holocaust survivor in 2019 at Birkbeck University in London who described her deportation from the Debrecen ghetto all the way to Mauthausen concentration camp in Austria. We are now at a point where not many survivors can testify anymore because most of them have passed away sadly so I firmly believe that carrying the testimonies and evidence forward to the next generations is indispensable. That includes the important task to still look and find perpetrators, collaborators and names of survivors who have not been identified until now.

I know that a journey to Auschwitz is tough and very sad but I urge everyone who ever visits Kraków to make the trip because the lessons learned on that day will remain invaluable for the rest of my life. I will probably come back at some point with my daughter when she is grown up and old enough to understand.

Needless to say that the football match I attended that evening had next to no meaning. The anger did not go away that night. The only positives I remember was to see Cracovia Kraków's ground and a decent level of distraction from the horrors I saw that afternoon. At least it gave me the chance to return to normal life to some degree and I remember talking to a golf fan at half-time who I think was English and appreciated my Ryder Cup 2012 polo shirt I was wearing at the game. To remember these little and in fact meaningless events were evidence to the fact that I needed some time off mentally from Auschwitz.

Some people who read this part of the book will probably ask themselves if I dedicated a chapter to Poland because I feel guilty or ashamed of the German occupation and the genocide. It is not that easy to answer but there is no personal guilt, of course, because I have not lived at the time. First and foremost, I feel ashamed as a human being that this was allowed to happen. However, as I mentioned earlier, these events need to be addressed, remembered and acknowledged as part of German history so it adds a bit of personal gravity. When you see signs all over the camp in German language it certainly raised my anger level possibly due to the fact that I could imagine better what kind of people were in charge because language is an important tool to recognize someone. Things like different German dialects, different conversations and decisions are easier to imagine if you speak the same language. However, my appreciation of Poland during my football travels had fairly little to do with any guilt or shame. I am interested in history and what happened between 1939 and 1945 is crucially significant, but I am also a firm believer in distinguishing between past and present. Both are very important and connected to each other but I am also able to meander around cities like Kraków, Poznań or Warsaw without constantly thinking about World War II. I also grew up after the Wall fell so even Germany as a divided country was a thing of the past to me because by the time I got interested in history a united Germany was self-evident. Of course, when you pass Poznań's town hall the first thing that comes to mind are Himmler's 'Posen speeches' which are highly important historical audio recordings about the genocide and are basically evidence enough that there should be no Holocaust denial whatsoever, hence, it has crucial historical significance. Also, when I was in Warsaw I thought at some point how devastating its destruction must have been including the scenes of the Uprising. Connected to those events, it is quite remarkable to remember the Warsaw genuflection in 1970 by back then West German chancellor Willy Brandt. Brandt was born under the name Herbert Ernst Kahl Frahm and was a social democrat who emigrated to Norway soon after the Nazis gained power in Germany in 1933. Obviously, being the chancellor in 1970 he was representing Germany in Poland and therefore, representing the German past as well but Willy Brandt was an anti-fascist fighting the Nazis in exile who in the end had to apologize for the crimes his enemies committed. In Polish eyes he was just another Nazi which underlines the sticking reputation of post-war Germans even for the ones who had actively resisted or emigrated Germany after Hitler took over. I have seen the knee fall a few times—obviously it happened way before my time—and it is one of the most important acts in post-war German politics.

The World Cup victory in 1954 was an important symbolic return of a democratic Germany into world society. It was a starting point really after the war but more important are the acts of the people like Willy Brandt who understood the responsibility Germany had to take—the full responsibility for that matter—to acknowledge all the details from the past in order to move on. Of course, the Warsaw genuflection was a symbolic act as well but to do it right in Warsaw considering Brandt's background is an extremely difficult and courageous act.

These are events that will always be present but I don't find it tough to enjoy modern day Poland and to interact with its people without constantly thinking about the war—and I don't see a reason why there should be a problem on that part. I enjoyed Warsaw and its Old Town on the day of the Europa League final 2015 with a friend of mine from Australia which was my second visit to the Polish capital. My first visit was a rather disappointing one because in the taxi to Legia's football ground I found out that no fans were allowed that day due to crowd trouble the match before so I ended up watching the game behind closed doors from the stadium pub. I have a habit of taking it a bit personal when I can't tick off the respective grounds I am attempting to see, so it will probably take a while before I will try again to see Legia Warsaw—but I eventually will.

There is no question that I will visit Poland again, on at least another four or five other occasions and without a shadow of a doubt, Majdanek and especially Auschwitz will remain the most important parts of my lifelong travels. There is a poster at one of the exhibition rooms in Auschwitz that quotes Hans Frank, a high-ranked Nazi and back then 'Governor of the General Government of Occupied Poland' which says: 'We need to free the German people from Jews, Poles and Russians'. It is not only a statement I could not disagree more on and when I passed that sign in June 2017 I was thinking: 'Who are you to dictate what people want or not?' That comment of a man who was eventually found guilty for crimes against humanity and was executed by hanging following the Nuremberg Trials taught me an invaluable lesson that I have lived by even prior to my visit to Auschwitz: Nobody has the right to tell me or in fact anybody who I should like and who I should hate…

Poznań Town Hall, March 2020

Cracow Gate of Lublin
Old Town, June 2019

Majdanek Concentration Camp Memorial

Memorial Shrine for an Unknown Victim

Chapter 8
The English and ze Germans

The relationship between Poland and Germany is an extremely sensitive one which is not very difficult to understand given the events I partly described in the previous chapter. Although I was born in a completely different time, I am still very careful on how to react in Poland if I ever come across anti-German sentiment. I never experienced such an incident to be fair, but I am willing to grant someone's anger simply due to the severe destruction that has been caused in Poland during the war and in many other countries as well. I would probably put it down to being part of the last generations that are familiar with 'Vergangenheitsbewältigung' (English: 'struggle to overcome the negatives of the past'). I don't think that anyone born in 1990 or later would really deal with this in modern day Germany. It is a difficult line to draw where collective guilt starts and ends but clearly, nobody carries the atrocities of ancestors with him or her. This prejudice has actually been an integral part of many European nations at least in fractions of their society such as the Netherlands, France or Great Britain. The idea that the Germans are fundamentally evil, no matter when they were born is something that carried over for decades since 1945 and in Britain it ended largely in 2006 only. Over the course of decades there were some changes and improvements but the mistrust of

Germans was quite deeply rooted in British society. Naturally, the world was in shock when details of the Holocaust and the German warfare came out and it was pretty clear no matter what will happen that Germany will have a long way ahead to be accepted again by most nations in the world. On this path there were many issues like the insufficient hunt for the perpetrators by both the Allies and West Germany, the (lack of) punishment of the German nation for World War II, also economically and the educational level regarding informing the people, and post-war generations about the Third Reich. After the Allies realized how many people were members of the NSDAP or to some degree involved, the denazification process was never really carried out to the fullest. The result was that large numbers of jobs in post-war Germany were occupied by people who had some sort of connection to Nazi Germany and a level of involvement even if they had just voted for Adolf Hitler. This is actually the origin of one of the oldest British stereotypes of Germany since the Second World War, the term 'Don't mention the war!' My mum was born in 1950 and her history classes could not be more different from my experience in school. She said when she had history classes nobody talked about World War II, reason being that the teacher was somewhat involved during the war. That's why there were very few conversations about it and it carried over to the post-war generations up until the German student movement in the 1960's where young people actively questioned the past of many Germans including their own family members in terms of their involvement in Nazi Germany. It did not change the fact though that at least until after the millennium, it was still widely assumed in Britain that whenever they talked to a German or travelled to Germany that the golden rule was to never mention the war. This to me is quite an astonishing fact coming from a generation that dealt with National Socialism in history class to an extreme extent. I started going to school just outside of Hamburg in 1990 and graduated in 2003 in Hamburg so overall, I would say at least five of those thirteen years the history content was the Third Reich only. Needless to say that it is heavy stuff to take in and I remember that some of the female pupils literally felt sick when we talked about a few details of the camps, the medical experiments and other forms of persecution including sterilization.

The difference between other countries who had suffered from German occupation was—and I say this very carefully— that the British always managed to keep a certain sense of humour on the matter which I found to be the right way to some degree. It is extremely difficult to really find an agreeable amount of wittiness around this subject but never intended to take away the horrors of what happened anyway, I would simply agree that Germans and especially Nazi leaders needed a certain level of 'revealing the ridiculousness' of the men in charge. I don't think there is anything wrong with it and I always felt like it was a good thing that somebody shows the mirror in Germany's face to reflect and to be critical of ourselves. Humour is surely a tool that is acceptable regardless of the seriousness that surrounds the entire subject matter because the mocking is directed solely at the perpetrators.

And the British loved another stereotype about the Germans that lived on for decades and that is the lack of humour. It is a prejudice I certainly cannot deny completely and I have not lived in the 60's or 70's to say that there was some sort of truth about it. From a German point of view, I was surprised how early people were actually joking about Nazis in public—although it did not seem to be the norm at the time. There is video footage that dates back to 1973 where comedian Johnny Burchardt fooled the audience at one of those German carnivals events by unexpectedly animating the crowd with 'Sieg' and large parts of the crowds almost accidentally replying 'Heil!' Burchardt then responded: 'I can't believe it, so many old comrades attending here tonight'. I think there are two things that are quite clear when it comes to the British making fun of the Germans. Firstly, I think a sense of humour in any circumstance of life is a good companion and it certainly helps to get over tough times and endure dark days. I am convinced it played its part for the British to have won the war and to have stayed strong because despite the fact that the battles in continental Europe were more devastating and cost more lives, the Battle of Britain and the carpet bombing of German cities were extremely severe air raids just like the bombing of Coventry or Dresden. This being said, of course, the Germans have a sense of humour which has been quite adequately explained by Henning Wehn who remarkably managed to have a career as a German comedian in Britain. It is simply a matter of significance which status sense of humour has in society, and clearly in Great Britain it has a much bigger standing and is a much more important trait. Moreover, although all these stereotypes have been fading and people have realized that some of these prejudices do not reflect the reality, I completely understand to keep the banter alive and to tease the opponent a little bit which was always the case when England played Germany in football. In the past it was more serious and surely the clashes at the World Cup 1990 and the respective European Championships in 1996 and 2000 were quite fierce battles, but it always remained an extremely one-sided rivalry with a much higher significance for the English. A lot of countries that played Germany at major tournaments with a strong animosity against Germans projected the German players at least to some degree with Nazis. Poland, the Czech, Denmark, France, England, the Dutch and other countries all had certain fixtures where it was a topic. To be honest, I think I am even emphatic enough to understand it. I am not sure how hyped up I would get if I was to play a German team in a big match and the team pre-match meeting would include footage of Wehrmacht soldiers marching into my country. I certainly would want to beat those 'Krauts' as well accordingly. There are only two problems that come along with that type of attitude. First, the German players knew what was going on. I get the anger of the opponent when playing Germany, but a player who was born in the 1960's, for example, and is compared to a Nazi will certainly want to win as well. A good example is the rivalry between Germany and the Netherlands which still exists to this day, but has essentially gone down to a pretty low level over the last ten or fifteen years. When Germany played Holland at the World Cup 1990 the rivalry and hatred was at its height. I don't know what went on in the Dutch dressing room before the game, but it could not have been more anti-German, I would suspect. German manager Franz Beckenbauer said after the match that he knew how desperate the Netherlands were to win this but quote: 'So were we!' It is pretty easy from a German point of view to revert the anger and hatred when you are constantly compared to a Nazi and that effectively includes to be consistently referred to a mass murderer—especially when you are born at any time after the Second World War. I never personally experienced this kind of accusation, at least not in a serious manner, but it can't feel very good. The entire scenario mounted so badly that Frank Rijkaard decided to spit at Rudi Völler twice in that game. I don't really want to bring up the old stories of Rijkaard or Batiston, it all has been talked about over decades, but just imagine it would have been the other way around and Völler did this to Rijkaard. I don't think that Rudi Völler would have ever been able to leave Germany to visit another European country. And I simply don't think that Völler deserved this, he was a fair sportsman and quite frankly, none of them players deserved to be compared to fascists.

The World Cup 1990 was the first football tournament I watched and it really triggered my passion for football. I was six years old and I do have other memories of that time such as my first day at school, learning how to swim or my first football training session but the World Cup is still fresh in my mind with a few highlights and it was certainly the starting point of having my own experiences as a football fan. I do remember the Germany v Holland game live on television and I knew something was wrong when the Rijkaard incident happened but I was too young to understand the rivalry and the historic context between the two countries. The same applied to England because only a few years after the semi-final in 1996 at Wembley I found out how desperate the English wanted to beat Germany. My first memories of Great Britain were thoroughly positive so I never really came across any resentment which is very different from the Dutch where the Rijkaard/Völler situation was a very early memory although I never felt any resentment against the Netherlands either. In school, I started to have the first English language lessons when I was ten. It was a voluntary class before it got mandatory one year later. I do remember it quite clearly because it was in 1994 and one day we had English class the day after the World Cup final. Unfortunately, due to the time difference with the final being played in California I was not able to watch it and just heard the next morning that Roberto Baggio had missed a penalty and that Brazil won. Later on in school, there were always topics about London, the Beatles, Big Ben and the famous double-decker buses that I started to like Britain at a young age without really thinking about it. I think because apart from very few pupils who learned French first in West Germany, England always had a positive standing in Germany because we were able to speak the language fairly early—if you were keen to study and to do your homework. The Euro 1996 was an extremely popular tournament because of the traditional stadiums such as Old Trafford, Villa Park, Anfield and of course, Wembley, and due to a certain familiarity because we have learned about English cities and traditions in school as part of learning the English language. I don't remember anyone ever talking badly about the British apart from the stereotype that they all have bad teeth which was obviously more banter than anything else. The semi-final against England I remember very well and not at all as a rivalry. The fact that an English newspaper declared football war on Germany, that a Russian student would get stabbed that night in Brighton for mistakenly assumed to have a German accent and the random destruction of German cars in London are things that I would only read about years later. The memories I have from that night is that it was an extremely hard-fought battle, a pathetic celebration by Andy Möller after putting the final penalty in the back of the net and a hedgehog that appeared in our garden which I fed somewhere in between extra-time and the penalty shoot-out. I never really sensed that I or any other German football fan wanted to particularly beat England. Again, it was always a very one-sided rivalry. I watched the match again just recently and I noticed how badly both wanted to win this match on the pitch though. The war must have been a topic at some point in the English dressing room and once again, just like against the Dutch, the German players responded to that stereotype. If you look at the celebrations after Andy Möller decided this match you can tell that the team spirit of this German team was excellent and the animosity of the opponent strengthened that. There were certainly a few incidents in that game where German players got kicked and the desperation of the English players to finally beat the old enemy again pushed the Germans who had to play without one of their best players that day, Jürgen Klinsmann.

Of course, there were times when England were on top. Euro 2000 saw Alan Shearer deciding the match with a header and quite remarkably both nations ended up not making the knock-out stages. The German national team needed a major overhaul at the time which only happened prior to the World Cup 2006. The first time I really realized that beating Germany meant everything to the English was the 5–1 victory in Munich 2001. It was also the year when I visited the United Kingdom for the first time. In March, I attended the Premier League fixture between Tottenham and Coventry at White Hart Lane before returning to Great Britain again in September that year to see Scotland face Croatia at Hampden Park in Glasgow (both with my dad). It was the same day England hammered Germany at the Olympic Stadium in Munich. The game in Glasgow ended around 4.50pm'ish and we took the next available train back to our hotel in Edinburgh from Glasgow Queen Street. By the time we arrived at Waverley station the match in Munich had started and the taxi driver told us on the way to our hotel that the score was 1–1, I think that's what he told us although I don't remember it exactly as I was not used to the strong Scottish accent back then. When we switched on the television in the hotel room England had just scored the second goal and the rest of the night took its course— one of the biggest victories in English football history albeit was just a qualifier. From then on, every time I would speak to an Englishman the first thing they would mention would be that 5–1 result and I would see t-shirts remembering that score for many years to come whenever I visited England which I did many times after. It only really stopped at the World Cup 2010 after Germany beat the English 4–1 in Bloemfontein which clearly marked the rise of the German national team again who would end up beating Argentina 4–0 in the quarter-finals, losing in the semis to Spain and eventually winning the World Cup four years later in Rio de Janeiro. There is also a significant change that happened in between that 5–1 score in 2001 and the 4–1 in 2010 and that was influenced by the World Cup 2006 hosted by Germany. That tournament marked a clear change of attitude by the English towards the Germans. The rivalry still somewhat stayed alive but it was the first time that large groups of British people travelled to Germany and it appeared to have ruled out most of their prejudices. There were parties everywhere, drinking on the streets, police with a hands-off approach and a nation that was extremely happy to welcome the world. The World Cup was such a success that Dutch supporters got rid of their orange Wehrmacht helmets they had brought to Germany to provoke but even they enjoyed themselves to the fullest. International papers later wrote that this was the first time Germans really felt a level of pride since World War II and to a certain degree it was very true. I can only remember that I felt happy because of all the people from all over the world enjoying their time so much and appreciating the country including all the positive attributes it stands for. I have to admit though that a lot of the so-called pride established in those four weeks was mainly just celebrations on the fan fests without thinking too much about patriotism really. At least that was my impression at the time.

However, 2006 changed a lot and put all the old rivalries and serious resentment to bed. Some international journalists would later repeat the statement when Germany won the World Cup in 2014 that the country could finally show some pride again. In that case I would disagree, it might have been correct for 2006, but Germany 2014 and subsequently nowadays is a completely different country. It is well advanced in multiculturalism and diversity and the German squad of 2014 is one great example. The old Nazi image of the opponents does not even work in the sense of banter anymore. When Jerome Boateng passes the ball to Sami Khedira who moves the ball forward to Mesut Özil and eventually Miroslav Klose scores there is simply no place and time anymore for any reference to Nazi Germany—and that is a very good development. I noticed it just recently when Holland met the Germans in Hamburg to play a European qualifier in 2019. One of the Dutch players, I think it was Memphis, got into a heated argument on the pitch with German defender Jonathan Tah. I am sure Memphis thought about saying something anti-German but I could see for a split second that he had to realize that Jonathan Tah is one of many Afro-Germans and that the old hatred simply does not work anymore. A multicultural Germany obviously bears a risk that also has to be addressed and that is the rise of right-wing views by people who simply don't want the country to be diverse. Diversity is a process that luckily nobody will be able to stop but the migrant crisis starting in 2015 and a horrendous World Cup in 2018 which resulted in the fact that many blamed out of form Özil for the failure, plus the issue that he took a photo with Turkish president Erdogan prior to the tournament. Now, there were loads of issues and mistakes at the time that subsequently caused a bit of a right-wing movement at least in parts of German society and at least to the degree that right-wing parties would get more votes. From a football point of view, it was inevitable that Özil's photo would backfire if Germany did not perform well in Russia. The big mistake was that the national team did not stick together, Özil made a mistake, yes, but he was still part of the team and never got the support by the German FA and eventually retired from international football straight after the World Cup.

For the British and many other foreign travellers, 2006 would become the starting point to see Germany differently. The appreciation has changed completely to the degree that stag-do's in Berlin, Hamburg or Munich are common destinations now, German christmas markets have become trendy and even German football is much more appreciated. Terraces, affordable ticket prices and beer at every corner made the fan fests from the World Cup 2006 live on to this day. English comedian Al Murray once said that making fun of the Germans paid off his mortgage and in a more recent feature 'Why does everyone hate the British?' he called the Germans 'wonderful people' which underlines the huge turnaround of perceptions and in times of Brexit more and more British people move to Germany and apply for German citizenship even—unthinkable twenty years ago. Of course, we are far away from an ideal scenario and I am hoping that these extreme views on German mentality will fade at some point. First of all, we are facing hatred and discrimination all over the world, the attacks in Hanau near Frankfurt in 2020 and the mosque shooting in Christchurch (New Zealand) in 2019 were as alarming and horrifying as the anti-Semitic attacks in Pittsburgh and Halle. There is still a lot to do in order to tackle racism and as long as political parties try to divide societies there will always be a danger. Therefore, I am careful with these extreme views on every country especially when it comes to highly populated nations like Germany or Great Britain. These countries have diverse demographics with historically greater volumes of immigration and emigration. The diversity of modern day Germany simply means that it is not that easy to categorize a country in such a one dimensional fashion. Germans are not all 'efficient', 'hard working' and 'intelligent'. Some really are but that does not rule out the fact that there is 'laziness', 'inefficiency' and 'stupidity' just like in every other society as well.

It sounds straightforward but on a number of occasions I talked to people who either had an extremely positive perception or entirely negative attitude towards Germans and not a whole lot in between. Certainly not all Germans are racist which some thought would be an accurate opinion even decades after the war, possibly because it was both convenient and due to lack of knowledge. Every now and then I see British rolling their eyes and saying about the Germans: 'Oh dear, will they ever learn?', whenever a racist incident happens in Germany. This is a statement I partly agree to be honest, because anyone in Germany and in fact the whole world who has not learned from World War II is basically a hopeless mind.

The problem is that the image of the blonde, blue-eyed racist German is a thing of a past, it simply does not reflect modern German society at all anymore. I mentioned before that there is a significant Afro-German community and the diversity and the progress of German life is something not everyone likes. Would it not be easier to just get reconfirmed if Germans behaved like animals like in the beginning of the 20th century in Namibia, or in Leuven in World War I or during most of World War II? A lot of countries could then keep hiding their own problems when it comes to racism and antisemitism. It obviously takes a bit of reflecting and willingness to learn if a country has changed and when old stereotypes do not make sense at all anymore.

I remember a video once posted by British Marathon runner Mo Farah who got pushed away by a security man at Munich Airport because Farah was filming with his phone camera inside the security controlled area. He then commented live on his phone: 'Sad to see racial harassment in this day and age, 2018 #airport #germany'. The footage shows nothing but a federal police officer doing his job but it was an attempt to straight away go along with the old stereotypes. This incident happened on March 6th in 2018 and made the headlines in both the UK and Germany. One day prior to that incident video footage was released of racist chanting at Nottingham University which I am sure not too many people have heard about. My point is that with all the problems that Germany still has to deal with, it is never good to characterize a country to an extreme level, we are not all 'wonderful', but we are certainly not all 'racist' either—by no means. Racism remains a global problem and it needs to be addressed in every country and history has to be mentioned and acknowledged as it happened, it is something many countries are struggling to admit. I think it is certainly something European nations have to address in much more detail to protect minorities.

The advantage of Britain is a longer history of immigration with a larger number of generations that settled into the United Kingdom over centuries. Berlin, the Ruhr Valley and other parts of Germany certainly do have a long span of immigration (over centuries) but in my opinion the Commonwealth and also a city like London are something Germany does not have on the same level. Considering the immense power the British Rule (including suppression) once had, its spread over the globe and the fact that both World Wars had been won naturally creates a high level of competitiveness and a sense of 'leading the world'. Considering the devastation of World War II there might be a bit of irritation that Germany is still around as a strong country. Margaret Thatcher once said that she did not want German unification and added 'We beat them in the war twice, and now they are back'. It greatly underlines a long lasting mistrust and disbelief that Germany recovered from World War II especially economically which is highly connected to the Marshall Plan carried out by Americans, a financial aid program both Great Britain and Germany benefited from but eventually, the West German economy experienced an incredibly high boost in the 60's. I think to this day the 'British Empire attitude' has never really fully ceased to exist and it was also part of the Brexit vote—certainly by the elderly voters. I think it is a combination of things, the wars and the fact that Germany returned to world society, economic factors and ultimately, the record between the English and the German national team at major football tournaments due to the importance of association football in both countries. I think it is also due to the fact that England is much more able to emphasise on their history and that the glory days lie in the past. Surely, there are dark chapters in British history which are starting to be addressed stronger now but there is no doubt that there is a much deeper cut in German history from 1945 which resulted in Germany seeking progress and talking about the future much more.

If we look at it from a sports perspective, the emphasis on history and tradition is embedded in British life. Wimbledon is a good example, the first Sunday of the tournament used to be a day of rest even if that day was the only day without rain the entire week. It also took quite a while before the Centre Court and Court No 1 experienced some refurbishments. History and old customs have always been a nudge more important in Britain because it represented the Empire and its strength and glory. Of course, there is a long German history as well although, the country only became united in 1871 but it used to be the so-called 'country of the poets and thinkers' with writers like Wolfgang von Goethe, Friedrich Schiller or Thomas Mann and a significant relevance to classic music. This reputation changed in World War I and subsequently even more drastically when the Nazi party took over. People sometimes forget that the country was also divided for fifty years with a totalitarian state in the East, an extremely significant chapter in German history as well. Progress, making up for the past and basic human rights certainly have a crucial meaning in German life and to keep the peace in Europe is essentially important. Needless to say that it is something that all European countries are aiming to keep (more or less), but the British view is a different one and I partly understand it, albeit I am a firm believer in the European Union and the idea of it. Germany might constantly remind Europeans that the EU is holding us together as a continent, but it is a different angle in Britain, a country that used to lead for centuries and being the ones who made the decisions. I can at least see why it is tough for older English generations to see Germany leading the way and emphasising on 'we need to keep the peace in Europe'. Of course, German politicians know the importance of it, but Germany was the country who destroyed the peace in Europe in the first place so other countries might be a bit critical or at least see other priorities. That's why I think the Brexit decision was more an emotional decision especially by the older generations rather than a rational vote. And that's why Germany is much more often in the British minds than vice versa.

I have travelled Great Britain quite extensively especially

around England and the struggles in parts of the country are greatly evident. And the glory days of the war are for some the only thing the people have left. I once travelled to Burnley to see Burnley FC play Middlesbrough at Turf Moor and I was in a pub pre-match with two Boro supporters. I noticed an elderly man at the bar who I assumed to be around seventy-five years of age. It was not difficult to realize that he had been drinking for decades and I was afraid that he did not have many years left on his watch. He had all sorts of different badges and pins from the Royal Army on his jacket and he kind of reflected the issue in England in quite a clear manner. The two World Wars won will always stand for the Allies and rightly so. It should be celebrated as often as possible marking the victory over Nazi Germany and the liberation of the European continent. However, it does not solve the current problems of the country and this old man with all this pride was simply left alone in this pub with arguably very little support by the government. He lives in an economically struggling city that never recovered from unemployment and outdated industries. The benefits he receives must have been on a bare minimum which I suspected he spent entirely in that pub. Apart from a few exceptions, mainly in the south anyway, the money is based in London and this type of economic imbalance cannot be any good for any society and that's why changes and moving on are good impulses for any country including the United Kingdom.

In contrast, Germany—understandably so—have been looking to move on from the past fairly quickly. In West Germany and then later on as a unified country, resentment against other countries in Europe just would not have helped in order to make progress and Great Britain has always been seen as a pleasant place to go and in fact, a close post-war ally. The old pubs, music, the flair of London and other British cities were always appreciated and to be respected. Apart from that it really is the case that the British do not really play a big part in day-to-day life in Germany. Al Murray once said on his visit to Hamburg: 'They (the Germans) do not really mention us much and if they do it is in a fairly positive way which is quite annoying'. I think that sums it up to the degree that some German football fans would not mind at all or even say 'it is about time' that England win their second World Cup or their first European Championship. The perception is generally very positive, quite contrary to the English view on Germany up until 2006.

And then there is media coverage and tabloids that for a long period of time forced the anti-German attitude because it was a seller and it worked in England. In Germany that kind of publicity would not have worked because the English were never considered the old enemy or in any way a big rival.

In 1996, when England played Germany in that famous Euro semi-final I was too young to be aware about how the British media loved the bashing of Germans and all the stereotypes that existed. 'England declares Football War on Germany' was one of the tabloid's headlines which I read about years later and resentment like this was barely seen or known in Germany partly because nobody cared and partly because the Germans could not do anything about it anyway. At the end of the day, there are extremely mixed opinions on Germans and it definitely depends on the time you have lived and met them. For example, I find it astonishing how positive the Russians generally think about Germany considering all the deadly and shockingly devastating battles in both World Wars including Stalingrad and the Siege of Leningrad.

What I also remember from the 90's was that perception that

Germans are naturally pessimistic, always a bit worried about what could go wrong which probably annoyed the British further because Germany had done well on several different levels such as the football national team, economically including the competitive automobile industry and just generally was seen as a country that should be much more grateful considering how destroyed it was in 1945 and where it ranks these days. And yet, the Germans still seemed to be too pessimistic. The English were much more positive in that regard and caused crushing disappointments with their own national team because the Three Lions have utterly underperformed in most World Cups.

However, the English always seemed to find a bit of pride which rarely existed in Germany over decades. The documentary, 'One Night in Turin' shows a small bit of footage of people leaving work early to make it home for the kick-off for the semi-final of the World Cup 1990 where confidence seemed quite high that England would win over Germany. And it was a bit typical that at the end of this film documentary about the English national team at the World Cup 1990 in Italy narrator Gary Oldman said: 'Maybe the best team won, but England had the best story'. In hindsight easy to say but probably correct that Germany had the best team of that tournament. But England had the best story? I think a country that just experienced the fall of the Berlin Wall and de facto reunification chose the best time by far to win a World Cup and it is an extremely unique story.

In 1996, it felt like England's confidence was through the roof on home soil and once again, the Germans won on penalties. 2010, when both countries met again at a World Cup it was even worse. The pre-match analysis on BBC was probably the worst prediction I have ever heard of. The pundits were so confident about the individual strength of the English team that they were completely blown away at half-time and subsequently post-match when the result was 4–1 to the Germans. Yes, Lampard's disallowed goal went down in history and it would have been a different game at 2–2 but regardless, Germany should have been 4–2 up by half-time and completely controlled the second half. I watched that BBC analysis about two years after the World Cup in South Africa and I was quite amazed how poorly the pundits had analysed the German team. They were basically surprised how good Mesut Özil was playing and at the time was clearly going to be a big player. That fourth goal Gareth Barry got completely outplayed by Özil and pundit Lee Dixon came to the fairly late conclusion after the match that Özil was a class player England 'haven't got'. This level of over-confidence and also lack of opposition analysis resulting in the mentioned crushing disappointment on a regular basis and Alan Shearer added on BBC 'If the Germans are watching us now about what we said pre-match they must think we are mugs'. This is something that rarely happens in Germany. There would be a lot more analysis, benchmark and worry about what could go wrong, almost like a 'glass half full v glass half empty' attitude. Over the years that has changed a bit, I think younger generations including England manager Southgate indeed assess what is happening in other countries also to learn from it rather than the old days of British exceptionalism and this refusal to take advice from continental Europe. I think it is connected to the historical aspect of it and also with England being on an island that they tend to do their own thing more than other European countries.

Fortunately for the Three Lions, this has changed which includes many factors. One being that the majority of managers in the Premier League are foreigners these days and I think the English national team and Gareth Southgate were able to get a lot of input from that. José Mourinho, Pep Guardiola and Jürgen Klopp are managers to name, and the latter to me is the best example of the healthy relationship between England and Germany these days. Klopp arrived in 2015 where the rivalry and all the hatred went down to a minimum. The English national team had their own issues for a while, they did not qualify for the Euros 2008, lost to Germany at the World Cup 2010, lost in the quarter-finals of the Euros 2012, did not make it past the group stages at the World Cup in Brazil 2014 and eventually lost to Iceland at the Euros 2016 which was considered a disaster. Things looked pretty grim and I recall living in West Hampstead when England faced France in their first Euro 2012 fixture. The reputation of the national team was as bad as it gets and when I passed a few pubs about thirty minutes before kick-off I could not tell that England were playing—it was that dead quiet. I think England needed a lot of redevelopment and change of thinking to improve, and experts said that the new training centre at St George was established way too late to keep up with the big nations. Things are now improved, there is an extremely exciting youth crop of players coming through and the World Cup 2018 was obviously a bit of a turning point for the English national team.

Prior to Russia, there was also an overhaul needed from a managerial point of view in English football and I think Jürgen Klopp with his attitude and ideas were a great asset to the Premier League. And it doesn't really matter where he is from, he is a bit nerdy, a bit crazy but a nice guy and happened to be German which really seems secondarily important. Clearly, things have changed which had its origin in 2006 with Germany hosting the World Cup. That major tournament surely altered Germany's reputation which should not shy away from the fact that from

Trautmann to Klopp there have been a number of personalities that shaped new relationships between England and Germany. It was not the easiest thing to do, although, I am not too sure if people really give it that much thought these days anyway. The German Empire, the years in between wars and Nazi Germany— in a sense these times are very far away from modern day Germany and I know the sensitivity of this statement because any shock waves from far right that sometimes come up need to be taken seriously in a democratic society.

Nowadays, the relations between England and Germany have never been better because it is not the media or politics that dictate how both countries get along but it is the people. British citizens travel to Germany regularly and vice versa, they communicate and exchange thoughts and ideas. I think never in history do British people know more about Germany, its geography, customs and mentality than these days. And most people know, just like Britain, that it is a country too diverse to really come up with simple stereotypes which is a thing of the past.

There is a lot to improve in Germany, no doubt at all. For the past ten years I have been a guest in my own country because I have been living in London and it is very interesting to observe what has changed and what still needs to change. We are a multicultural country that needs to protect our minorities and some people might have a problem with it, but the benefit of a diverse, open Germany is undeniable. I am not the most patriotic German, but at least I want my country to do well for its people and be kind to others which probably includes a bit of patriotism. Inevitably, people should always be critical of their own country especially to those in high-ranked positions politically, economically and its progress of integration. There seems to be a problem with civil courage at times and radical parties are still trying to divide the country, at least there are attempts and these are areas to improve on and there is a chance to learn from other people rather than believing tabloids or politicians. I think generations after me who are even younger have understood that already. I have certainly noticed more often than ever that young English people are wearing jerseys of the German national team and at the same time, it is common to see football fans in Germany in Arsenal, Liverpool or England gear. I think the younger generation will be the ones to keep Europe united—without prejudice but with a duty to remember the past.

Chapter 9
The addiction to sport

I mentioned earlier that football travelling includes several different passions that make me plan trips, study fixtures lists and flight deals almost non-stop. The constant feeling of wanderlust, a desire to see football matches in exotic countries and a collector's passion to complete certain leagues, federations or continental associations. Roughly fifteen years ago, I realized that only supporting my home club was not enough anymore and I decided to see all sorts of random football matches world-wide, no matter how far or what tier. A youth game in Iceland, a women's fixture in New Zealand, a third place match in Chile or a lower tier fixture in Canada, any fixture that would work with my travel plans I attended. This level of ticking off football grounds seems insane to people who do not have a relation to football or sports. And then you have the regular football fan who has a season ticket for his football club and maybe attends a few away games per season. These kind of supporters understand groundhopping but they struggle to comprehend watching a game as a neutral and to some degree I get their point. Of course, if I follow my team the match itself has much more meaning than a random fixture, but still the above-mentioned passion and the desire to tick off new grounds is so relevant to me that I keep going with the lists of stadiums I would still like to see. On the other side of the scale you have these crazy groundhoppers who basically travel all year long which is an amazing financial and timely effort. I met people who have seen every ground of the top two or three leagues in Thailand or Vietnam and other countries which even for me sounds a bit too much. It is quite an unbelievable effort if someone is actually able to see a match in all 211 FIFA member countries which is something I will surely never achieve, mainly because of the fact that I do not only follow association football.

In recent years, probably ten or twelve years ago, I realized that football travelling is not enough and I started to attend many different sporting events. I grew up in Germany where football is such a dominant sport and a lot of athletes of other team sports are complaining that football is too powerful when it comes to salaries, media coverage and simply its standing in society. Very rarely do other sports really compete with professional football. There was a time when Boris Becker was a tennis star, when the German handball national team won the World Cup or when the German ice hockey team unexpectedly won the silver medal at the Winter Olympics. These are usually short-lasting moments because football in Germany is by far the biggest sport. In other European countries it is similar but at least there is a bit more competition like rugby in France and Great Britain, cricket in England or basketball in Spain and the Balkans. What is interesting to me is how different sports are compared to football and what different types of experiences occur when attending various sporting events. It is once again also a collector's passion because there are certain events I want to see once in my lifetime such as the Super Bowl, the Stanley Cup in the US or the AFL Grand Final in Australia. I have started to become a bit annoyed when someone who is interested in sports can only relate and talk about his own team or country so I tried to at least get a bit of knowledge on all sorts of different sports. Especially when travelling to so many different countries it is very beneficial in order to communicate with people. I remember once sitting in a sports bar in Las Vegas in 2005 and talking to an American about the Dallas Cowboys and how they are still considered to be 'America's Team' despite the fact that they had not been any good for quite some time. A few weeks prior I attended the NFL game between the San Francisco 49ers and the Cowboys at Candlestick Park—the former stadium of the 'Niners'—and thought about that topic. If I did not have any interest in thinking about reputation, size, fan base, success of other teams in other sports I would never have the opportunity to talk about sports with so many people on my travels. The first time that I got interested in teams and leagues outside of association football was in the mid-nineties when American sports started to get covered on German television. I do remember hearing about the National Hockey League when I was a teenager probably because a lot of people knew about the Mighty Ducks of Anaheim, so I started looking at teams and played hockey on the PlayStation. The first big hype and the first time I remember that basketball really dubbed over to Europe was obviously Michael Jordan and the Chicago Bulls.

That kind of team dominance in a sport and a player being so much better than anyone else was clearly a global sensation and as a twelve year old it was completely new that instead of playing football in the park we bought a basketball and went to a basketball court to shoot hoops. German television started to broadcast live games to show Michael Jordan on TV and also because of Detlef Schrempf, a German basketball player who back then played together with Shawn Kemp and Gary Payton for the Seattle SuperSonics. I even remember owning a Schrempf jersey and I got a bit taunted for that because everyone had a Jordan jersey in sports class, obviously there was no comparison whatsoever between these two players on the quality of play. At the time it felt impossible to ever attend an NBA game in the United States but the interest for ice hockey and basketball went on and off over the years. Nobody in Europe really followed the NFL at that time. There was the NFL Europe at some point with actually some good attendances but it would never be a league that could compete with association football, just like 'soccer' never really competes with American football or baseball in the United States.

In 2005, I spent three months in Washington State to complete an internship as part of my business studies in Hamburg. My initial plan was to spend the summer in Los Angeles but a friend of mine from the USA recommended to stay in the Seattle area instead as he highly rated the city and the state—an advice that turned out to be extremely valuable as I enjoyed my time in the Great Northwest very much. This was the moment when I got into the NHL, NBA and NFL and at least tried to get to know the franchises better. I even followed baseball a little bit as my internship was in the marketing department of minor league team Tacoma Rainiers but I am very far from following baseball on a regular basis. The first thing I did when I arrived in Seattle was—guess what?—attended a football match or 'soccer' as it is called over there. The Seattle Sounders were playing English side Sunderland AFC at the impressive Seahawks stadium which that night had been more or less empty. Soccer in the northwest has changed a lot over the last ten to fifteen years because the Sounders, Portland Timbers and the Vancouver Whitecaps are playing in front of decent crowds these days. At the time though, soccer really was unpopular in the States and considered a 'soft sport'. I have to admit that the pre-season friendly that evening was a shocker and not much happened so the few people who attended started to boo some fifteen to twenty minutes before the end of the game. I did attend a few more fixtures in the US such as the Portland Timbers and the San Jose Earthquakes at home but I soon realized that I had to get interested in other sports that are more popular because soccer games over there were pretty uninspiring at the time, simply due to low attendances and poor level of play. The only thing I remember from the Timbers match I attended was mascot Timber Jim, a guy who was running around the touchline with a jig saw which also seemed to be the highlight for most of the spectators—although Portland thrashed Atlanta 6–1 that day. The rest of the evening I spent learning about Oregon's microbreweries and meeting a group of pretty annoying Austrians and Germans in one bar who smart-assed a lot. In San Jose—a city I would visit fourteen years later with my wife to see the San Jose Sharks in the NHL—I was impressed by a woman whom I asked for the way to the stadium and she replied: 'You know what, I can drive you there'. This was quite nice considering I was a stranger and also a little bit surprising to me.

My first NFL game was the earlier mentioned clash between the 49ers and the Cowboys. This was a completely different experience from some rather dull soccer games which included my difficult attempt to make it to Vancouver which I explained previously in this book. The pre-match vibe at an NFL game certainly is something special with its tailgates, the music and the gatherings. Game day is a proper holiday for some die-hard fans and as a young man it was quite an exciting experience to see these two traditional franchises meet up, both on five Super Bowl wins and with big fan bases. A couple thousand Cowboys fans made it to Candlestick Park around lunchtime, smoking cigars outside, drinking beer and loads and loads of taunting. This is a big difference to football in Europe where the away fans are located in separate sections and are usually escorted to the ground by the police. The violence factor is simply bigger whereas in pro sports in the United Stated it is more about teasing the opponent and there is no separation between home and away fans in the stadium. One guy I remember to this day seemed to make it his duty on this Sunday afternoon to just keep taunting. Every time his Dallas Cowboys made relevant yards or threw a decent ball he turned to the 49ers fans and made a weird stance. It was like the last jump in high bar athletics at the Olympics when you land on the ground and stay steady to get the highest amount of points. He made this stance every time the Cowboys came closer to the red zone and it obviously annoyed the home supporters. I think in Europe at some point he would have either been punched in the face or kicked out of the stands, although, in American football and ice hockey, fights do happen fairly frequently due to a high amount of alcohol consumption. Beer in North American stadiums and arenas is a topic for itself because the prices are ridiculous. I think the highest I have ever paid was in 2019 at the Los Angeles Rams. A can of Bud Light was prized at eye-popping $ 16.

I was on a lower budget in 2005 though so I did not bother anyway to purchase much in the stadium but that game in San Francisco was the starting point of attending NFL, NHL and NBA games on a regular basis. A few weeks after my journey to California I was due to fly home to Germany in October of 2005 and I had a one night stopover in Chicago. The National Hockey League had not played for a whole season due to a lockout which happens when the NHL and the NHLPA (the players' association) do not sign off a Collective Bargaining Agreement. It meant that the Chicago Blackhawks had not played at the famous United Center for a while—which is the same venue Michael Jordan made history in the 90's and where his statue represents his achievements outside the arena. As I did not have my accommodation sorted that evening, I went straight from Chicago O'Hare Airport to United Center with all my luggage and my match ticket for the Blackhawks game against the Mighty Ducks of Anaheim, now called Anaheim Ducks. First, I thought they would not let me in with two big suitcases but the security guy was very friendly and cooperative. When he saw my Seahawks souvenir football in my suitcase he said: 'Ah, here we go, just travelled from Seattle?' After a pretty disappointing Blackhawks performance and a 4–1 defeat I had to pick up my luggage after the game and still needed to sort out my accommodation. It must have been around ten'ish at night and I still had about a twenty-three hour layover ahead of me. When I left the United Center with my suitcases and two more bags, a guy spotted me and asked if I needed any help. In a big city like Chicago you never know if the intentions are always good but I told him that I needed a taxi to an affordable hotel and that I am just having a stopover. Not only did the man walk me to the nearest taxi he also recommended a motel that was only a few blocks from the Sears Tower and the Hancock Building which was such a helpful and nice gesture that from this day on I became a supporter of the Chicago Blackhawks, a franchise that would later become a dynasty with Stanley Cup wins in 2010, '13 and '15 including an incredible celebration that took place at Soldier Field, home of NFL side Chicago Bears. In fact, in 2013 I returned to Chicago to see the Blackhawks again, finally the

Chicago Bulls who at the time were playoff contenders but nowhere near the Jordan era and the Bears who were playing the Baltimore Ravens on a rainy November Sunday in a game that had to be interrupted due to a storm over Chicago. I really appreciate the passion of this city for sports and it is a great place for food and bars. In the midst of experiencing these sports events in the US I started a quest: Attending every venue of the NFL, NHL and NBA at least once. It means that I cannot revisit too many places as there are currently 93 teams in those three leagues combined and a busy schedule for me accordingly. A few teams share the same venue but it is a lifelong goal that will take an uncertain amount of time. As of 2019, I have covered just over a third and time-wise I am able to tick off a maximum of three to six franchises per year. When I featured on a local television station in Philadelphia I calculated that it will probably take me another twenty years to achieve this high stake goal which sounds a realistic time frame. There are pro's and con's that come along when doing stadium and arena hopping in North America. The positive thing is that all professional leagues are 'closed leagues' which means no promotion or relegation so there are barely any new teams. The only possibility that a team adds to a league is a new franchise to be founded which will happen in the NHL by 2021 with the Seattle Kraken joining the league. The negative side is that American pro teams build new stadiums on a regular basis. I decided that attending one match of the respective team is enough as I can't possibly revisit a franchise every time they build a new arena.

Like in every sports league I come across very traditional teams with a bigger fan base and clubs that are smaller and less significant. In the NHL it is fairly simple that the first teams that formed the league, the 'Original Six', represent the origins of franchise hockey. Those teams are the Montreal Canadiens, Toronto Maple Leafs, Boston Bruins, Detroit Red Wings, New York Rangers and the Chicago Blackhawks. The different locations in North America are quite significant in my opinion on how well-supported a team appears to be. Canada is a hockey-mad country and by far the favourite sport over there. There are nations where a higher population and a strong affiliation to sports results in countries doing well at various sports just like the United States, Great Britain, Germany, Spain and Australia. In Canada it really only matters that the hockey national team wins Olympic Gold (also on youth level) and which team wins the Stanley Cup, one of the most prestigious trophies in all of team sports. I remember Canada winning Olympic Gold on home soil in 2010 against the United States including Sidney Crosby's deciding goal to this day because they were showing live pictures of Vancouver's streets straight after the deciding goal. The scenes were very similar to a European or South American nation winning the World Cup, it has an identical meaning.

Looking at the two Canadian franchises of the Original Six, the Toronto Maple Leafs and the Montreal Canadiens, they have a very interesting history. The Maple Leafs have a huge fan base in Canada, which goes even as far as Newfoundland, and incredibly, they have not won the Stanley Cup since 1967. The city is so desperate to win a title again that nothing can really make up for it until the Leafs win the trophy again—not even the NBA title for the Toronto Raptors in 2019, simply because basketball is nowhere near hockey in Toronto. I was impressed how filled the Air Canada Center was on a regular season night against the Minnesota Wild considering it is 81 games before the play-offs start. On the same trip I made the six-hour bus journey from Toronto to Montreal to see the most successful hockey team in the NHL. The Canadiens have won the Stanley Cup a staggering twenty-four times. When you walk around the Bell Centre in Montreal with a church being not far from the arena I could feel the history and the success of this franchise straight away. Similar to the Maple Leafs, the big years are over for the so-called 'Habs' but at least they managed to win their last Stanley Cup in 1993 so the drought is not that long compared to the Leafs. It might have just been a personal observation but in Montreal I could tell how big the franchise is, I think in terms of records it would be fair to call them 'Real Madrid of hockey', but they seem more reserved about their hockey team than in Toronto. I was quite impressed how proud and loyal the Maple Leaf fans are considering they have not won anything in decades. In that regard, they are probably 'the English national team of hockey': loads of history, huge fan base, but no major title since the 1960's. Both of these Canadian franchises share a fierce rivalry with another Original Six team, the Boston Bruins. Traditionally, the east coast and the midwest of the United States are closest to the hockey passion in Canada really. Another city to name that is strongly connected to their sports teams is Pittsburgh. The Penguins are a force in hockey right now and they have one of the best ever players in Sidney Crosby. However, when talking about sports in Pittsburgh there is nothing bigger than the Steelers. When I visited the city in 2016 I noticed that straight away, the bridges that lead into the city, the skyline and the impressive Heinz Field that almost looks like the cathedral of this working class city hit hard economically by American standards. On NFL game day you see flags everywhere saying 'This is Steelers Country' and the fan base really is a nationwide one. I strongly hope that the Steelers do not build a new stadium anytime soon because Heinz Field is a wonderful venue. It is that iconic that it featured in the movie 'The Dark Knight Rises' where villain Bane blows up the stadium—fortunately, it is just a film…

The only negative I remember that day was another ticket incident which really only matters for passionate collectors. There is an error on my ticket that says 'Pittsburgh Steelers vs vs' instead of 'Pittsburgh Steelers vs New York Jets' which quite frankly still bothers me a little bit. Regardless of this 'First World Problem', I enjoyed Pittsburgh a lot because it is a working class sports town so I was happy to tick the Steelers and the Penguins off my list—one great stadium and one decent arena. One story I have to add on the Penguins was that I was attending a pre-season match and almost did not make it. The game was part of a school event for kids in Pennsylvania so tickets only went for sale to local schools. Luckily, there are always touts in the US who want to make a bit of extra money so a guy who was waiting in front of the school buses asked if some pupils did not show up and if there were any spare tickets. In the end, he had about twenty tickets in his pocket and sold them for twice the price which was outrageous but I was happy to pay the $ 40 because the other option would have been to come back to Pittsburgh at some point which is not that easy when you have about sixty-five North American venues still on your list.

Some venues in other parts of the country can be extremely dull just like in Europe as well—when you want to complete a league there are always three or four grounds minimum that do not have the hostility or fan base. I remember when I was in Phoenix (Arizona) to see the Coyotes versus the Detroit Red Wings that the arena was half empty and the majority of fans who were at the game were Red Wings supporters—most likely people who had moved to Arizona from Michigan due to better climate or job opportunities. Florida Panthers are another example of usually low attendance although it is different between regular season and playoff games and also, in the United States the attendance always rises with success. Winning trophies is so much more important compared to Europe which is quite a significant difference between the two continents. Finishing second or third of a major tournament is still a reason for European teams or countries to celebrate and to remember wins on the way to a final or semi-final. In the US being runners-up is pretty much as bad as getting knocked-out in the early stages of the regular season or playoffs. It is a very different approach to things and I would say that short-term success is even more relevant in North America than it is in Europe. It obviously has something to do with history and mentality. The competitiveness of the society to be better, stronger and richer is part of the DNA of the United States and including two World Wars won makes it kind of mandatory that only finishing top counts. I remember when former United States national team coach Jürgen Klinsmann said that winning the World Cup for his team would be an unrealistic target. That caused a fairly decent amount of outrage amongst American journalists. Whether Klinsmann intended to just motivate his players with this statement or this being just an honest assessment I don't know, but it just highlights that if you don't go for the ultimate prize in any sport representing an American team you might be in trouble. Needless to say that the United States were light years away from winning the World Cup 2014 when Klinsmann was in charge but I get the point that any country who participates should aim to win it all or to at least try and win every game. Boston is a good example when it comes to 'winning mentality' because the New England Patriots are a dynasty that won six Super Bowls since 2001 which is extremely difficult to achieve in a highly competitive league—arguably the toughest league in all of pro sports. What I admire about the mentality in the United States is that constant desire to win trophies, one big prize is not enough. The New England Patriots stayed hungry during the Tom Brady and Bill Bellichick era, which just came to an end with Brady leaving for the Tampa Bay Buccaneers. It felt like the first title was as important as their sixth Vince Lombardi trophy. This is quite different in Europe apart from a few examples. Yes, Manchester United, Liverpool, Real Madrid, Barcelona or Bayern Munich have won multiple titles in a row but in European football there seems to be an earlier sense of satisfaction when titles have been won multiple times. Of course, other teams shape up and the desperation of beating a dynasty grows and grows over the years, but winning more than one title seems to have a bigger meaning in the United States than in Europe. A major trophy means a bit of a cut or a mission completed instead of thinking 'let's try to win it again next year'. At least a few percent might be missing. The most drastic example in Europe was the German national team in 2018. Clearly, there was a sense of satisfaction already having won the World Cup in 2014 and there is a history of defending World Cup champions performing poorly the following World Cup. France, Spain, England and Italy had experienced that as well and the attitude of the players clearly is a major factor. I do not think that it would happen to a franchise in American sports. New England for me is the most recent example, a team that always shows up and when they come short in Super Bowls, which happened despite their six Super Bowl wins, it is because the opponent was just stronger on the day but certainly not due to lack of attitude or commitment. Winning never gets old or boring and Boston sports teams represent that. It is a city that takes a lot of pride in their pro teams, just like Chicago or New York. I noticed that when I attended a Boston Bruins game at the legendary TD Garden and in many of the great Irish pubs in the city. The Irish background of this city is quite remarkable and although I love Dublin, I think Boston would be a perfect Irish city.

TD Garden brings up good memories as I watched my basketball idol Dirk Nowitzki play for the second time. At Madison Square Garden in New York—possibly the most famous arena in the world—I saw Dirk in action in 2007, but in 2010 when I was in Boston Nowitzki was about to reach the height of his career which ultimately resulted in winning the NBA Championship in 2011. As mentioned previously, it is really difficult in Germany to get much appreciation outside the association football world because football is such a dominant sport. It also means that in other sports the funding by local associations, clubs or nationwide federations is much lower. It is quite difficult to become a superstar outside of football when you are German. It was remarkable to see this guy from Würzburg become one of the best shooters in the NBA and that night at TD Garden he put on a very good performance including a 99–90 win over the Celtics. In 2011, the Dallas Mavericks and Dirk Nowitzki won the NBA title by beating the Miami Heat, LeBron James and Dwayne Wade in the Finals. I was watching the playoffs including the 4–0 sweep of the LA Lakers at home and subsequently, the final game of the finals series somewhere in Denmark as I attended the U-21's European championships in association football that summer with a friend of mine. Certain sporting events just like Dirk's championships are so special that I always remember where I was watching it. In the end, you can't just focus on one sport only.

I have recollections of watching Wimbledon in Tokyo following an Urawa Red Diamonds fixture I attended in 2013. In Durban before an African Cup of Nations fixture I sat in a bar following the Australian Open and a big memory is being glued to a large screen in a pub in Kilburn, London, when Europe turned the tide at the Ryder Cup 2012, to this day one of the biggest comebacks in sports. These kind of memories and following different sports is almost like learning a new language to interact with different types of sports fans including significant differences from continent to continent.

On the day I attended the regular season game between the Montreal Canadiens and the Buffalo Sabres in the NHL I sat next to an Australian policeman from Melbourne who had participated in a police exchange program of the Commonwealth. He spent a few weeks in Montreal to share experiences and duty with the local policemen and then later on Canadian police staff would travel to Australia to do the same he told me. Clearly, when I started talking to him he was not too fond of hockey as there is very little coverage about it in Australia. The ice cold wind that day in Montreal was another thing he did not like too much but generally, he really appreciated his time in Canada. The conversation turned out to have nothing to do with hockey as soon as he found out that I graduated from Bond University in Queensland and that I followed Australian Rules football (AFL) at the time and even played a little bit at Uni. When I arrived in Australia in 2008 I had never heard of 'Aussie Rules' and I was actually prepared to watch a lot of rugby while down under. I learned that sports fans particularly from the state of Victoria are not into rugby but Australian Rules football. I therefore discovered a new sport due to my flatmate being a loyal supporter of the Geelong Cats in the Australian Football League. It gave me the chance to give this policeman a bit of a 'being at home' feeling by talking about Australian sports. It could not sum up my addiction to sports more that I was sitting at Bell Centre in Montreal, having a beer and randomly exchanging thoughts about a sport popular in a country that is more than 10,000 miles away. As he supported Carlton I was aware that the biggest rival of this guy's team (I do not recall his name) was Collingwood and he simply loved to tell me how much he hated Collingwood Football Club.

Unfortunately, apart from a few association football matches and the big rugby clash between the Wallabies and the All Blacks, I missed out on attending an Aussie Rules league game in Geelong due to a rather extensive drinking session in Melbourne and not making it on time until kick-off. I was lucky enough to also spend a month in New Zealand and helped organize a FIFA event in Christchurch, a city that eleven years later would experience a traumatic right-wing terrorist attack.

There is a connection between Canada and New Zealand when it comes to dominating a sport or at least setting new standards on a regular basis. In Canada it is hockey and in New Zealand it is rugby. To be honest, when I attended the Bledisloe Cup in Brisbane it was mainly because of the famous 'haka', the game itself was secondarily important. The 'haka' is certainly the most unique pre-match custom in world sports albeit I have a mixed opinion on it. It is supposed to intimidate the opponent which works in rugby because the All Blacks are an extremely strong force in that sport, probably an edge stronger than the Springboks or Wallabies in the southern hemisphere. In other sports it might turn out to be an embarrassment to perform the haka and then get heavily beaten by forty points or so in basketball or by six goals in association football.

The All Blacks are a global brand though with its silver fern and three won World Cups. Without having a rugby background even I noticed straight away the meaning of the national team for New Zealand. And I love the respect that is deeply rooted in the sport of rugby. Association football is the sport I grew up with and will always be 'my sport' regardless of the fact that I try to follow as many different sports as possible. However, there is no doubt that modern day football is facing a huge amount of issues that sports fans do not like. Diving is probably the most significant disgrace in football and the respect between supporters and particularly referees in rugby is quite remarkable. Fans of different teams get along and even if it is a fierce rivalry like Australia v New Zealand or Scotland against England the respect seems to be preserved at all times. No mass confrontations on the pitch and the on-field referee is always able to explain his decisions to the players in a professional, calm manner. In football, players and sometimes managers do not seem to have a whole lot of respect for the referees in heated situations and on the other side in rugby referees never come up with a 'one man show' just because they are 'in charge' which is something association football should learn much more from. I noticed that there is more communication between teams and officials of different sports nowadays though, just recently sporting directors of the German Bundesliga travelled to California to get some input from other teams such as the San Jose Sharks in the NHL. I find this a very useful development in a global sports world to interact in between different team sports.

Generally speaking, there are different objectives when attending a sporting event. In most cases it is seeing a new ground, very often it was following my home football club or my desire to complete the leagues in the NFL, NHL and NBA. The 'haka' is certainly a special reason and simply some events have this special kind of aura or vibes to it that are unique. I would say when it comes to an unexchangeable type of atmosphere regardless of hostility, capacity or meaning it is Wimbledon. On a nice summer day in south London with the history, the perfect cut grass and the Centre Court it is a place I will return to many more times. I once queued up for roughly seven hours to see Roger Federer, one of my all-time idols, and I enjoyed every minute of it. There are these kind of sporting events when time seems to stand still and only the 'now' counts. Wimbledon and the Wimbledon final in particular are one of those events in which a highly significant trophy is up for grabs. The Super Bowl or the World Cup final are similar events but the level of history, the style and the uniqueness are second to none for an annual event at Wimbledon. Of course, the World Cup and the Summer/Winter Olympics can have a higher meaning because it happens every four years only and then there are teams who have not reached a major final for such a long time such as the Kansas City Chiefs in American football or the Boston Red Sox and Chicago Cubs in baseball. The Super Bowl or the Olympics are ever changing venues though and Wimbledon has always been at the same place and to me it is one of the most iconic sporting events in the world. There is a reason why Wimbledon and the Wembley Stadium stand for tradition more than any other venue for someone who grew up in Germany because of Boris Becker at Wimbledon and the 1966 World Cup final at Wembley.

This is why attending sports venues is an invaluable experience in comparison to watching it on television at home. The Tour de France had that vibe but it went downhill when the doping scandals went through the roof and when a guy who won the tour seven times turned out to be one of the biggest cheats in sporting history it is tough to keep the beauty of an event alive. I used to follow the tour quite closely prior to its downfall and I don't think it has ever really recovered from it.

I am also struggling a little bit to follow Formula One on a weekly basis. In the 90's it was obviously extremely popular because Michael Schumacher was a superstar and broke every record. I was not really a fan of his but growing up in Germany it was a huge topic and I decided to at least once attend a Formula One race. Most people would probably pick Monaco which must be an iconic circuit to see live, also the history of Spa in Belgium is special for this particular motorsport. Schumacher raging after David Coulthard and colliding with him on that rainy Sunday in 1998 is certainly something I still recall watching on television. For me personally, my more realistic options to attend were Hockenheim or Silverstone and it turned out to be the latter due to the close proximity to my flat in north-west London. The first thing I realized is that the guys who work at one of these food and drink booths must go nuts after a weekend of Formula One considering the noise level and very little ear protection to process all orders as quickly as possible. Silverstone certainly has its history but it is nowhere near other historical sporting venues in the United Kingdom. I have not grown up with the sport of cricket which probably applies to many countries outside the Commonwealth but I did attend an England cricket international once at Lord's Cricket Ground and without having too much connection to the sport I could tell the historical significance of this venue and having lived a certain amount of time in Australia I do understand the passion for it but similar to baseball, it is a sport I simply have not followed enough. It is quite important to have an early connection to a sport in my opinion, that's why I follow tennis much more, for example. The heydays of Boris

Becker, Stefan Edberg, Pete Sampras, Andre Agassi and Michael Stich are still fairly fresh in my mind and I am extremely lucky to live in a time where Roger Federer, Rafael Nadal and Novak Djokovic put the entire sport to another level.

I recently attended the 'Vierschanzentournee' ('Four Hills Tournament'), a very traditional ski jumping event taking place in Austria and Germany and the history of this event was present as well to me although, when you are from northern Germany you don't necessarily have a close connection to ski jumping. I was impressed how many international fans from Poland, Britain, Norway or the Netherlands 'invaded' the small city of Garmisch-Partenkirchen that New Year's Day in 2020. The scenery of such an event is simply breathtaking.

And then there are the rather 'odd' events such as the PDC World Championships of Darts at the legendary 'Alexandra Palace' in London. I started following darts a little bit between Christmas and New Year's even before I moved to the United Kingdom because it was live on German television and there is traditionally not too much on in continental Europe right before the end of the year. I attended an evening session at the so-called 'Ally Pally' in 2013 just to see the best ever darts player Phil Taylor. I lost a bit of interest in recent years but the times of Phil Taylor, Raymond van Barneveld, Wayne Marble or John Part I followed for a few years. At the Darts World Cup there is one priority for the fans; partying. People get dressed up in all sorts of crazy outfits and party all day long. It sounds fun in theory, but you also spot some people who are looking for a fight after a few pitchers of beer or liquor. What I will never forget was a very tall and strong 'Shrek look alike' in a playful cow costume. After a few hours of drinking he decided to stand on a table looking for a possibility to get into a brawl. Luckily, it turned out to be fine, but it is fair to say that attending a darts event usually turns into a proper drinking session without paying too much attention to the event itself. It might have changed over the years but it is basically a big Christmas party in a venue that really is considered one of the most traditional ones in London and certainly worth a visit.

Speaking of tradition, the Golf Majors and the Ryder Cup are tremendous sporting events without having played a decent amount of golf myself. The first time I realized that major golf events have a special aura to it was the Ryder Cup 2004 with the winning putt by Colin Montgomerie. I basically only followed the Ryder Cup until 2010 before really getting into the Majors. The day Europe won the cup in 2010 was my first day at work in London. Due to rain, the Sunday session of the Ryder Cup had been moved to Monday and I was basically following the day during my induction in my office in Camden Town. Needless to say that golf is a pretty big sport in Britain and the 'Miracle of Medinah' in 2012 is one of the greatest sporting comebacks I have ever seen. That Sunday session when Europe turned the tide was simply incredible and I decided that day that I will be attending the following Ryder Cup 2014 in Scotland. I managed to get a ticket for the Sunday session at the historic Gleneagles golf course which was an interesting experience. I realized that a lot of sports fans attended the event who like golf but come from other sports backgrounds just like myself. Association football fans, American football fan bases and guys who just like being part of a big sporting event and having a few beers. I had to laugh when I saw an American tourist near the golf course who seemed to have spent the entire day in the on-site pub in front of a television. I am sure he could have done the same back home in America without spending money on flights, hotel and Ryder

Cup tickets…

What I like about the golf majors, the Ryder Cup and the tennis grand slams is the style these events express. The Ryder Cup, Wimbledon or Augusta have a certain uniqueness to it. The quality of play is just remarkably high. Some major finals in team sports are sometimes not the most exciting or at times not even the highest quality events. Occasionally not even the best teams make it to the finals especially in association football. In golf majors or tennis grand slams one can be sure that the quality of play is outstanding. And it is the character and passion of individual sports that have some magic to it. Ian Poulter on fire at Ryder Cups or Justin Rose's incredible birdie putt on the 17th hole in Medinah against Phil Mickelson, these are moments when a sport is at its pinnacle. Rafael Nadal winning the French Open thirteen times or Roger Federer's epic battles at Wimbledon against Roddick, Murray, Djokovic or Nadal, the sport has been on another level since these players burst onto the scene. I was lucky enough to see Rafael Nadal at the Australian Open 2008 in Melbourne which was fairly coincidental because I bought my daily ticket and flights before I knew who was playing. Having attended several Wimbledon tournaments, the French and Aussie Open, I am certainly keen on completing the tennis grand slams one day in Flushing Meadows to see the US Open.

Chapter 10
Rivalries

Every sports fan has at least one team he dislikes to say the least. It is a clash between two sides where the league table does not really matter and the result of the fixture completely defines the mood of a fan and the level of mocking he has to endure in weeks to come. Rivalries can have different backgrounds and reasons, some are short-term; others have been existing for centuries. The most common origin of a hatred rivalry is the close proximity of cities or clubs, in Europe known as 'local derbies'.

Manchester United v Liverpool in England, Dortmund v Schalke in Germany or Atalanta v Brescia in Italy are classic examples of rivalries between two cities located close to each other. Similar are bragging rights in the same city. Two of the biggest city rivalries I can think of in association football are Celtic v Rangers in Scotland and Boca v River in Argentina. Both also have a religious meaning because Celtic are a traditional catholic football club whereas Rangers have protestant roots. And in Buenos Aires it is fair to say that River Plate and Boca Juniors really are religions in itself, the results in those derbies are simply crucially important for day-to-day life in Glasgow and probably even more so in Buenos Aires. I attended the so-called 'Old Firm' between Celtic and Rangers at Celtic Park in 2011 and a goal for either side is as good as it gets in Europe when it comes to celebrations.

Another factor of rivalries are wars that have been fought between countries and regions. It mainly applies to national teams but can also relate to different counties or domestic states such as Yorkshire and Lancashire in England. Leeds United and Manchester United share one of these rivalries although it has been a while since Leeds have played in the first tier of English football, prior to their promotion in 2020. World War II was certainly a conflict that has carried over to football in numerous countries as explained previously, mostly countries that had been occupied or attacked by Nazi Germany. This is fading though due to younger generations coming through and simply times have changed in Europe.

There are certainly some fierce rivalries in south-east Europe such as Turkey against Greece and domestic derbies in Istanbul and Athens, for example. One of the more recent wars in Europe that took place in former Yugoslavia certainly shaped various very tense fixtures. Serbia v Croatia is a hatred rivalry that exists pretty much in all sports such as football, tennis, basketball, volleyball and even water polo. There is this interesting phenomenon that expatriates tend to be more patriotic compared to living at home which caused a few brawls at the Tennis Australian Open in Melbourne—a very multicultural city and a country with a fairly significant Serbian and Croatian background population. This has caused a few fights pretty much on a football level at the Aussie Open.

One of the most famous rivalries in association football is Real Madrid against Barcelona, which is both due to the success of both teams in Spain and Europe and the tension of different regions with a high significance historically.

Barcelona is the largest city of Catalonia, a region that

recently tried to detach itself from Spain with an independence vote and Madrid is the capital in the heart of Spain. It is not only a rivalry of different regions but a significant historical divide due to the Spanish Civil War. The nationalist regime of Francisco Franco fought the Republican faction which included the territories Catalonia and the Basque region and eventually took over the power to turn the country into 'Francoist Spain'. So Real Madrid v FC Barcelona is in many ways 'El Clásico' and both clubs traditionally attract one of the best players in the world which makes it one of the highest quality fixtures in the European football calendar.

In US sport, rivalries do less often have their origins in close proximity between two teams. Of course, the east coast has plenty of cities nearby, much more than the west coast, so Boston and New York is traditionally a big city rivalry. I do not have a strong baseball background, but I know that the Red Sox and Yankees share one of the oldest and biggest rivalries in sports. In the United States they love their superlatives and even domestic league title winners are called 'World Champions' but in the case of the Red Sox and Yankees it really is a hatred that is known by most sports fans world-wide. That's why—without being a big baseball fan—Fenway Park for a Red Sox v Yankees game is still quite high on my bucket list. I don't necessarily take sides for every rivalry, but in this case I would cheer on the Red Sox because the Yankees logo has become a bit of a global fashion brand without people who are wearing it being aware that it actually stands for a baseball team and not only for the city of New York.

I have been to New York and Boston a few times and I do like both cities and it is a city rivalry with a lot of tradition. I do not have a connection to either the New York Rangers nor the

New York Knicks but Madison Square Garden is an arena every sports fan has to attend at least once in his/her lifetime. I don't use the term 'iconic' too often but when it comes to the MSG it really describes the arena. It is an incredible venue right in Manhattan and its wooden roof construction inside the building makes it distinctive.

For a groundhopper it is possible to follow a rivalry without necessarily taking sides. I do have my own team I support which is an association football club I grew up with and naturally, I have rivals I don't like and teams I want to beat. Once, I watched a documentary about sectarianism between Celtic and Rangers and in one sequel a German Rangers fan called Celtic fans 'fenian bastards' just because he decided to take on Rangers' side. To me that is pathetic. That guy was not from Glasgow, has not grown up there and all of a sudden adapted all that hatred. I don't think that is the way to go. For example, I love the NFC North in the National Football League because of its rivalries but that does not mean that I take sides at the same time. The Green Bay Packers against the Chicago Bears is one of the oldest rivalries in American pro sports and I can honestly say I fully enjoy when both teams meet up, but I don't necessarily have a team I choose out of the two. The Packers and Lambeau Field represent all the tradition and the classic fan base of sports. The documentary 'America's Parking Lot' underlines how different the Packers' organization is set up compared to franchises who constantly raise ticket prices which makes it very difficult for die-hard fans who are not wealthy to attend games on a regular basis. In Green Bay the Packers are largely owned by the supporters.

The Bears on the other side are a very traditional team from the big city and Chicago itself is just a great sports town. This really is a game between two teams I could generally not pick sides. What is also different in the NFL is that the four divisions cause all sorts of different rivalries. If someone had no clue about the teams in the National Football League and would have a look at a US map on where the teams are located, that person would probably say that the New York Giants and New York Jets share a fierce rivalry, Pittsburgh and Philadelphia in Pennsylvania and the Rams and Chargers in Los Angeles. This is obviously not the case because rivalries really depend on the different divisions.

One deep aversion that really has interested me in recent years is the one between the Philadelphia Eagles and the Dallas Cowboys. When you start getting into the NFL, fan bases and rivalries within the divisions matter but not every division has the same tension. Each team of every division shares a rivalry because they want to make the playoffs (which are similar to the World Cup knock-out stages), but in some fixtures it is more than that. The NFC East is a very interesting division that recently has not presented the strongest on-field football teams but certainly the biggest rivalries. The New York Giants are a team with a large fan base coming from the 'Big Apple' with that special kind of New York self-esteem, the back then Washington Redskins (currently on a name change) are a huge franchise, very traditional with an immense number of supporters formerly known as 'Redskins Nation'. And then there are the Eagles and the Cowboys. Dallas is known to be 'America's Team' with fans world-wide which is connected to Super Bowl wins in 1992, 1993 and 1995 respectively. Their home stadium, the AT&T Stadium, is one of the most fascinating venues in all of sports with a very influential owner in Jerry Jones. The only problem for this gigantic franchise: they have not won anything in twenty-five years and even have a poor playoff record in the last two decades. That's why sports fans outside Dallas struggle to still consider them 'America's Team' and they are almost in a state of being a sleeping giant. In the documentary 'America's Parking Lot' one of the main Cowboys fans comments in one particular scene: 'I hate the Eagles so much!' and it made me wonder how someone can have such a strong antipathy towards a franchise that is over 2,300 kilometres away from Dallas. Obviously, they play in the same division which is a bit odd geographically to see Dallas from Texas in the NFC East. Moreover, there have been some extremely hard fought battles between the two teams for decades which shaped the rivalry. And there is one other significant reason for the hatred: the Philly fan base. Just like most cities on the east coast of the United States, sports has an invaluable meaning for the people and Philadelphia is no exception. The Eagles fan base is considered to be the most savage in the country. As mentioned before, in Europe away fans are usually located in separate sections especially in association football to avoid crowd trouble. In South America it is even more severe that for derbies away fans are not allowed into the stadium. In North America it is usually a bit more moderate so fights and brawls are more or less alcohol related and more individual cases rather than organized hooligan groups. One reason is that taunting is much more common in the United States and beating the opponent on the field is more important. This is a bit different in Europe where hooligans sometimes don't even care about the result on the pitch as long as they beat the opposing mob in a brawl before or after the game. Once again, winning has a bigger meaning in North American fan culture than it has in Europe to a certain extent. The NFL and even college football is extremely competitive and at a young age athletes are somehow drilled to win and tuned only to care about beating the opponent on the field.

The Eagles' fan base is almost like an Ultra European supporters group where wearing an opposing team's jersey could end up quite fatal. Dallas Cowboys fan gear is particularly dangerous but I have heard from many sports fans that Philadelphia is the roughest place to go. I once sat at a bar just outside the American Airlines Arena in Miami prior to attending the NBA regular season fixture between the Heat and the Indiana Pacers and I was talking to a bartender about fan bases and a Chicago Bears fan joined the conversation. When I mentioned Philadelphia the barman said that he once went to a game in Philly with his kids and that he got beer spilled all over him and his children because they were from Miami. Even to me, someone who has experienced rivalries in Europe and South America, it sounded extremely savage. I had visited Philadelphia once before I heard about all of that and revisited Philly in 2019 with more knowledge and the clear task to see the 76ers, Flyers and Eagles. It was a great experience because due to a short feature on a local television station where I talked a little bit about the Eagles and sports in general, a few people recognized me in food markets or at Lincoln Financial Field, home venue of the Philadelphia Eagles, so to some degree I became part of an Eagles fan base that has such a bad reputation. Contrary to all the bad reputation, I started to really like Philadelphia and their fans probably because they share the same love of sports. They simply appreciated my on-going quest to see every venue in the NFL, NHL and NBA. I remember talking to a guy who was making the traditional Philly Cheesesteak for me at the Bourse Food Hall who simply loved the purpose of my journey. In the end, sports fans truly are a family with the same passion. And you have to give it to the Americans, sports and winning trophies is an essential part of their confidence, pride and history. I felt that in

Philadelphia in particular.

The winning mentality is extremely distinct in American sports which starts early even in college. College football is competitive and there are some deep rivalries such as Ohio State against Michigan or Alabama versus Auburn to just name a couple. There is a proper hatred between the fan bases and the motivation on beating the rival is immense. I think the pressure level on these young players is stronger than in Europe which can have a negative effect on the mental side of a player. When I attended a Los Angeles Rams game in December 2019 at the LA Memorial Coliseum I had about three hours of time before kick-off to see the Rams tailgate first. On stage, a Rams promoter talked to four or five coaches of youth football teams and their development program. One of the coaches mentioned something very interesting. Youth level coaching seemed to have changed its opposition analysis and game plan approach. He said that coaches used to push the players so much into the direction of hating the opponent and to win at all costs. Of course, this is one idea but it can have a very negative impact on a young player in terms of pressure and also self-esteem if only winning counts. It seems like the approach has changed more to the direction that coaches encourage players 'to beat their opponent out of respect' so instead of hating a team it is now more about appreciating the rival and that it is more an honour to win the game. I think this fine margin is a much better approach to shape a young athlete and I think in American sports it is a valuable change in developing youth athletes. I remember these comments still fresh in my mind because I do recall when Dirk Nowitzki entered the NBA two decades ago that American basketball scouts were saying that he was probably 'too weak and too European' which I would consider a fairly insulting assessment. It probably suggests that Europeans from an American point of view do not want to 'win at all costs' or do not have what it takes in terms of 'winning mentality'. Considering the comments of these coaches prior to the Rams game it seems that the attitude regarding sports in the US and Europe is getting closer and closer and that there are more reference points in learning from each other. That's why there is more interaction between clubs from different sports and obviously there is also a marketing strategy behind it. That's why the NFL regularly hosts fixtures in London and the biggest European football teams go on US pre-season tours and Asian exhibition games. It is part of a globalization that is extremely profitable in professional sports.

College football has not dubbed over to Europe on a mainstream level which is probably comparable to lower league association football. I do know about the rivalries in pro sports in the United States and there is a bit I follow regarding college football rivalries. For instance, if I ever see an Alabama Football fan anywhere in the world I know that I have to greet him / her with a 'Roll Tide'. Regardless, the European fan base on following college football is still quite exclusive. It is worth pointing out though how big college football really is and that is very much competing with the NFL in terms of popularity. It is quite similar to lower league association football in Europe really. There are people in the United States who follow the Premier League and to a lower extent La Liga, Serie A and the Bundesliga. What a lot of people do not know overseas is how many big clubs now play in the second or third tier in front of pretty big crowds. Sunderland in England and Kaiserslautern in Germany are examples that come to my mind, two clubs that are very similar. Both experienced a pretty significant downfall as they were both relegated to the third tier which is remarkable considering the size of each club. The fan bases of both Sunderland and Kaiserslautern are huge and both have played a third tier match in England's League One and Germany's '3. Liga' (League 3) respectively in front of over 40,000 supporters. This high number of followers obviously mounts pressure to make it back to the top tier as soon as possible which is a difficult task considering the financial situation and when you are such a big club it can be tricky to really adapt and accept to play in the third tier of the football pyramid. What makes Sunderland and Kaiserslautern very unique is that football defines the mood and spirit of their city like nowhere else in western Europe. In cities like London, Paris, Madrid or Munich, for example, football is an important part for the people but there are other points of interest and football is just one piece of many in their social life. In Sunderland and Kaiserslautern the results of their local football team really means everything and has an extreme impact on the town's mood. Sports fans from outside Europe sometimes underestimate the meaning of lower tier teams and leagues for European football fans and in contrast, I tried to point out here for European sports fans how significant college sports is for the American sports community. The big difference is that leagues in Europe are 'open' with relegation and promotion and North American leagues are 'closed' meaning no teams can't either get relegated or promoted.

A former fellow student of mine from Hamburg who happened to study at the same university I graduated in Australia once asked me years after our graduation if I can organize tickets for Chelsea v West Ham for him as he knew that I had moved to London. This request came one day prior to the match so I was not able to get any tickets in such short-notice but I recommended to attend one of the various lower league teams in London as an alternative. His reply was: 'Nah, I don't follow lower league tiers' and I could not have disagreed more on this statement. Real sports fans will always appreciate fan bases who follow their team in lower leagues also because they are quite likely to watch some really dreadful football week in and week out. That's why I surely have some respect for clubs like Sunderland and Kaiserslautern because the fans keep these traditional teams alive who also struggle with some clueless owners on a regular basis. People who only attend the 'big games' in bigger leagues with the atmosphere possibly being worse than in lower league fixtures are condescendingly called 'fashion fans' and not true sports fans in my opinion. They are probably even worse than fair weather fans who only support a team in good times which is also something I cannot identify with at all. It is sadly very common in American pro sports if a team is not performing that the attendances drop drastically. It was quite astonishing how empty Washington NFL games were in 2019 considering their fan base and that touts were even struggling to sell tickets for a tenner, just because the team performed so poorly...

What also stands out at Sunderland and Kaiserslautern is that both have some fierce rivalries. Sunderland in the north-east are considered 'Wearsiders' and their biggest derby is against Newcastle United known as the 'Tyne and Wear' derby, one of the most heated derbies in England. Unfortunately, both teams do not look like meeting up for quite some time.

Kaiserslautern from Germany's south-west have several different rivals such as Karlsruher SC, Eintracht Frankfurt or 1. FC Saarbrücken. Their biggest derby though is against SV Waldhof Mannheim known as the 'South-West-Derby' which recently took place after both clubs found themselves in the same league for the first time since 1997. These games take place under huge police presence and it is quite a scene considering that it is not even a top tier league fixture.

The last derby I attended was on February 22nd, 2020 at the Volksparkstadion in Hamburg shortly before the world started to change immensely.

Philadelphia Eagles v New England Patriots, Lincoln Financial Field (November 2019)

Chapter 11
COVID-19—The dark ages

Today is May the fourth, 2020 and I am writing these lines in north-west London in the midst of the Coronavirus outbreak. The last time I used any type of public transport was on March seventh so pretty much two months ago. The last time I attended a football match was on March 3rd to see Lech Poznań at home. Shortly after, the first matches were played without fans; before, week after week, all sporting events got suspended. Since then, I have been following the sports news, of course, but with most matches being played behind closed doors and some leagues still on hold it is a likely forecast that attending another venue will take several more months. I completely switched off any groundhopping activity and went with the government guidelines here in the United Kingdom.

In Europe, the virus has hit several countries extremely hard, others to a lesser degree. A few nations just like Germany were in the lucky position that COVID-19 arrived in other European countries first. Obviously, the majority of governments and societies were unprepared but for Italy it was exceptionally hard as it arrived earlier with a rapid rise in infections and deaths. The spread went on quickly and there are many cities and regions world-wide that suffered in terms of health, losses of friends and family members and also economically. The city that comes to my mind regarding overcrowded hospitals, empty streets and simply the face of this pandemic is Bergamo in northern Italy.

Bergamo was the first European city that was covered on several media channels in order to make clear how severe this virus is impacting a region and community. I visited Bergamo in November 2017 and many sights that I saw on television during this pandemic I recognized from my visit.

It was a sunny day on the twenty-seventh of November when I arrived in the morning to check-in to my hotel in Bergamo. Due to the fact that I had all day before the evening kick-off between Atalanta and Benevento in the Serie A I decided to walk a few hours and check out the town. The interesting thing about the city of Bergamo is that it has its classic northern Italian city centre and then additionally, the so-called 'Citta Alta', an upper town which is part of the UNESCO World Heritage. It takes about thirty minutes to walk up there with a beautiful view and some very traditional northern Italian sights such as cathedrals, museums and a library. I recall Bergamo to be an extremely peaceful city that did have some violent events in its past, but in 2017 it really was a relaxing, historic place to visit.

The world has changed drastically since then and Bergamo stands a bit for the old Europe that has been hit hard by the virus. Life is not the same anymore and it will take time before normality returns and some cities might never recover. It is a deep cut in the history of Bergamo.

That's why I will always remember my visit to Atalanta, a football club with die-hard supporters that had recently made some headlines in the UEFA Champions League. I am not a virologist so I don't aim to analyze in detail what has been done or should have been done during this pandemic and I also realized straight away that professional sports was not important at all as soon as the virus spread. Games played in front of empty stadiums never appealed to me and it was somehow irrelevant to know the scores of the respective fixtures. Even the fact that the Bundesliga returned earlier than other major leagues did not bother me too much. What interests me though is to assess how football might look like in a post-COVID-19-era.

I followed the first St. Pauli match after the top two leagues resumed in Germany via radio for the first time in probably eleven or twelve years. It was quite nice and 'old school' to follow the fixture against Nuremberg on the St. Pauli radio channel from my bedroom where I still have a giant picture of the Millerntorstadium hanging above my bed—which is quite remarkable that my wife still has not asked me to replace it with a picture of our wedding but it will probably happen soon. Listening to a football match requires much more thinking than watching it live on television. You imagine the pitch, the formations of each team and where the players are positioned when having the ball. It is even more strange to follow what is going on with all games played in front of empty seats for the remainder of the season as there is no indication from the noise on the terraces. St. Pauli won the game 1–0 which was good news, but clearly, I seemed to care less these days. The feeling was not as euphoric as it was a few months ago. For example, I still feel a great amount of energy when I think of the 2–0 derby win over Hamburg at the end of February 2020. However, the meaning of the game has changed and other things are more important in this moment in time and rightly so. It will take time when things are back to normal and I have to admit I can't wait to be back in a packed stadium again no matter which stadium it will be. I think it will be a great and special atmosphere to return for the first time in five or six months.

However, professional sports need to learn from this unique situation. I am quite amazed how many big clubs are in financial trouble right now and the fact that organizations and franchises with big profit margins are struggling severely, indicates a lack of sustainability. This needs to change, expenses in modern football especially when it comes to salaries and wages can't go on like this and that might be the only good aspect from the business side of it that came along with this horrendous pandemic—a change of thinking on how to operate an enterprise, firm or football club. A lot of people have lost their jobs and there are many people and small businesses who will never recover from it which is nowhere near as dramatic as the health issues and people that perished but it is still a major concern. I live in one of the richest cities in the world and I am far from the shocking impact that this virus has on poor people, but the societies and countries that can't bounce back that quickly should be a warning sign that something has to change in our way of thinking and it is up to governments and large firms to focus on more sustainability and equality.

I get asked a lot if my passion for groundhopping has changed since the virus stopped all sorts of travel for several months. The passion is still there, of course, but I think it all did have a major impact. I will probably travel less in the future and I keep my bucket list that I have unchanged and won't add too many more grounds which I had done constantly before COVID-19. My last trip was due in March 2020 to see three new NHL arenas in Vancouver, Edmonton and Calgary respectively and I still have all vouchers after all travel arrangements got cancelled. I will still do this planned journey with my wife as soon as it is possible, but after that it will be a shorter list of destinations with bigger gaps in between ticking off new stadiums so ultimately, this virus did change my thinking already. And to be fair, the months during the lockdown that I spent with my family were a great experience to bond and return 'back-to-basics' which slowed down my life in a pleasant way.

Sadly, the killing of George Floyd in Minneapolis on May twenty-fifth added more anger and outrage to an already difficult time. Having watched the footage of the hate crime and the impact it had not only on American protesters but around the world touched thousands and thousands of people also in Europe. The incident certainly carries an incredible heaviness of American history with it and it is an on-going problem which has never been resolved in an extremely wealthy country where minorities have suffered over centuries. The societal and financial disadvantages also result in a huge health problem which was seen once again during the pandemic because the infected and death rates had a high toll on African Americans in the United States.

There is a tendency in America that people do not like to look at other countries or opinions of foreigners for many reasons (exceptionalism being one major factor), but there are still a number of people who want to listen, learn and progress. From a sports perspective, especially when it comes to team sports, I learned early that nationality, ethnic background, sexual orientation or social status does not matter when it comes to being successful, having team spirit and growing together. Germany is a very multicultural country in this day and age with still a lot of work and progress to be done but an even more diverse society are the United States and there is a lot to improve to minimize inequality, fight racism and ignorance and to reform its justice system which seems way overdue in certain cities, states and counties. Minneapolis was just another example that the old demons of hatred, racism and fascism still exist in modern society and one important key to end all this comes from privileged white people and younger generations who see the injustice, acknowledge it as such and are willing to change this together with minorities and persecuted people who have suffered for too long.

Città Alta of Bergamo (November 2017)

Chapter 12
South America

I consider myself an expert on the European continent. There are a few major sights that I have not seen yet but I have been to more countries, cities and regions than most people I know. I would even say that I have been to more places in the United Kingdom than most locals I have met in London and its surrounding areas. Travelling in Europe is convenient and easy so it does not require a high amount of risks to take. South America for me at a young age always represented the opposite compared to Europe. It was far away, dangerous and poor—partly caused by European intervention historically. When I was a teenager I already followed football globally so the Copa América was a tournament I occasionally watched when it was on. The atmosphere and the rather dull live picture quality always impressed me because it felt like an adventurous continent with people who love football even more than I do. Not that I planned early to visit South America, but places like Argentina, Brazil or Colombia had something fascinating about them even when I knew very little about these countries. Colombia had a bit of a bad reputation in the 90's but players like Higuita and Valderrama were such crazy football players that there was this fascination about it.

Argentina and Brazil always represent a long list of

outstanding football players so I feel a great sense of respect and admiration.

The first time I had the opportunity to get a feel of South America was in 2012 when I visited Buenos Aires. It is a city I fell in love with straight away: great food, full of life and extremely passionate football fans. South America is a pleasant adventure because it is so unpredictable, vibrant and the mentality of its people make it so liveable—despite all the issues most countries have on the continent. My first football experience was seeing Argentinos Juniors and the Diego Armando Maradona museum in La Paternal.

A few days later I was about to see one of the most famous clubs in world football: Boca Juniors. Me and a friend of mine were able to obtain two season tickets we could use for this match against Godoy Cruz as they were offered to us through a few contacts. We paid roughly fifty Euros per ticket – which was way over normal price – and we made our way inside the ground quite early. I think two hours before kick-off we were in the stadium and despite one minor scare it went fairly smoothly. We had a slight issue that the season tickets belonged to a die-hard fan who also had season tickets for his kids so a picture of one of his children was on the ticket. It resulted in a tense moment that a steward denied access first because obviously I was not the kid on that season ticket. However, one of the Ultras noticed what happened and told the security man that it is all fine and I got in.

When you are not fluent in Spanish things can get a bit tricky in Argentina especially for 'gringos', but I was impressed how nicely the Ultras of Boca treated us when we showed up on their terrace. Needless to say that everyone noticed that we were no regulars at the famous 'La Bombonera' but the fans we spoke to were quite impressed that we travelled all the way from Europe to see their team play. And to this day I think that experiencing a Boca Juniors home game was one of the best stadium visits I ever had.

I did see River Plate's impressive Estadio Monumental Antonio Vespucio Liberti as well, but it was for an Argentina international so the atmosphere was a bit more reserved and the stadium is located in a much wealthier area so it was a fairly easy trip to tick off my third Argentinian ground. That same trip I managed to see Montevideo, the capital of Uruguay, as well and of course, I was trying to attend a football match. Unfortunately, it turned out that it was impossible to go.

From Buenos Aires we decided to take the ferry on the Rio de la Plata. CA Peñarol were supposed to play the day after our arrival at the Estadio Centenario. Due to the fact that the national team had a fixture coming up in the national stadium Peñarol decided to play their league game in a different stadium. As we found out from a taxi driver the ground was located far outside the city in a rather dubious area. In fact, the driver advised us not to go in the first place but we thought that it can't be that bad. It was about a forty-minute drive and the closer we got to the stadium the fewer people and flats we saw and the bus stops more and more looked like a run-down mini shed. Inevitably, the fans that were on the way to the stadium noticed the taxi and wanted us to get out. First of all, probably nobody ever saw a taxi in the area getting to that particular football ground and secondly, we had the word 'gringo' basically written all over our foreheads and quickly decided to return to Montevideo's city centre to watch the game in a bar—in this case definitely the right call otherwise the locals would have taken all our stuff...

In 2015, I visited Chile for the Copa América which turned out to be a bit of an on-going drinking session with a travel companion who was not too much into stadium hopping. However, we still managed to see the third place match between Peru and Paraguay in Concepción after a nine-hour-bus journey from Santiago with an extremely bad hangover. We did manage to make it back to Santiago for the final between Chile and Argentina but we did not bother to try and get tickets after a tiring week. This is certainly something I would not do these days, it would be an absolute no brainer for me to attend the final as well.

Santiago de Chile seemed a relatively wealthy city to me with a number of bars and restaurants, Concepción had a bit less to offer but it was impressive to meet a local at the game who spoke excellent German when he found out we were from northern Germany. The guy said that he lived a few years near Stuttgart and was trying to move back as soon as he is in the position to do so. His German was nearly perfect and it was interesting that he had good knowledge of rivalries. He told me that Argentinian football fans are not very popular in South America due to their fanatic patriotism and that there are several chants between Chilean and Argentinian football fans in order to mock each other. I do not remember all of the examples he gave me, but he mentioned that Argentinian supporters have a song about Chile's country shape and that it is so small which makes it difficult to spot on a world map (in comparison to Argentina).

A couple years earlier I visited Colombia, the beautiful region of Antioquia and the stunning city of Medellín. Despite the fact that Medellín has two big clubs, Atlético Nacional and Independiente, I was not able to attend a match as it was over the Christmas period and the leagues were on its break. I did a stadium tour of the Estadio Atanasio Giradot with its beautiful hills in the background and I have heard many stories about the passionate fans of Nacional, a team once supported by no less than Pablo Escobar. I am yet to return to Colombia though for an actual match (just like Uruguay). Even a flight delay and an additional day in Bogotá did not help to find a match as I was leaving the country early in January of 2014. I will try to be back at some point because just like most countries in South America the people I met in Colombia were extremely guest friendly and there is this natural pride when foreigners visit their countries which is not fake but a genuine appreciation.

Having been to seventy countries it is tricky to name which one was my favourite because there are so many different aspects to think of. It is simply difficult to compare a country like Norway or Scotland with Colombia or Iceland with South Africa. However, if I had to name a country that highly fascinates me positively and negatively it would be Brazil. I don't think there is another country on the planet that offers such a diversity in landscape, its people and also in wealth and poverty. I might be a bit biased because my wife is from Brazil, but my two visits to this gigantic country have been simply amazing and full of great memories.

My first trip was in 2014 for the World Cup where a friend of mine and I managed to get tickets for three games in three different cities. The journey started in Rio de Janeiro which in my opinion is the greatest city in the world. The beaches in Leblon, the craziness of Lapa and the view from the sugarloaf certainly make it a very special place. At the renovated Maracanã we saw Belgium take on Russia in the group stages. There was a lot of criticism ahead of this World Cup that the money used to build the stadiums and to host millions of football fans should have been used for the needs of the people such as education and to fight poverty. Brazil is a very wealthy country with a huge discrepancy between the rich and the poor. The favelas are known all over the world as separate cities where the extremely poor and disadvantaged have to live under outrageous conditions. Obviously, as a tourist during a major tournament you don't get to see this side of Brazil too much and it did not feel right to visit a favela as part of a guided tour but I saw bits of the reality over the nearly two weeks I was in the country. The police presence everywhere was quite significant and I do remember watching Germany against Ghana at the fan fest on the Copacabana Beach where occasionally shots had been fired from a nearby favela. It is quite an ambivalent feeling to be that privileged and able to watch the World Cup on the beach when at the same time fights break out between police forces and rioting people who have been clearly disadvantaged their entire life.

Brazil is a country of extremes. On the one hand it has beautiful sceneries, amazing food and extremely friendly people and on the other side there is a tremendous amount of inequality, violence and murder on a daily basis.

For the second game in Salvador de Bahia to see Bosnia against Iran we flew from Rio to Salvador and when the plane started its descent we were flying over a sea of favelas for probably half an hour. Images like this certainly made me think about values and how lucky some people are and how bad the situation is for others. Salvador is an impressive harbor city known for seafood and dancing, the place is full of colours and life but I did notice being watched as a foreigner a few times. It can be a dangerous place and the World Cup certainly protected me a bit from possible violence or robbery due to more police presence. From the city centre, the so-called Pelourinho, it was possible to walk to the Arena Fonte Nova and the path included parts of a favela we passed on the way. There were people making music with drums (in Bahia called 'Olodum') for the fans which was nice to see, but I also noticed that it was all a bit forced and a cover up of the real problems in Salvador, a city with a predominantly black community who had suffered for centuries under slavery in Brazil. Once again, I realized the inequality and this tremendous heaviness of extremes that can be seen all over this huge country. It underlined the discrepancy in wealth even more that we could afford to have dinner at an excellent seafood restaurant where the portions were way too much for us knowing that people not far from the place were starving on the streets. I certainly learned even more how thankful we should be in western Europe to have such a privileged life and even more so that we have our responsibility historically in poverty especially in South America and Africa.

The last stop of the journey was the most eventful one in Recife. We had tickets for Germany against the United States. Well, we still needed to pick up tickets from a guy which turned out to be one of my longest days ever. Upon arrival in the state of Pernambuco we first needed to find our hostel outside of Recife in the historic town of Olinda. It was late at night when a clearly annoyed and tired receptionist tried to find our room in a small hostel filled with German and American football fans. After a long discussion we had to accept a room opposite of a defunct restroom including a pretty bad urine smell. However, after we saw that a guy was sleeping in a room with no door facing a forest we were happy that we could at least lock our room.

After a rough night with very little sleep I got up early and had some breakfast upstairs with various football fans ready for the match that would kick off at 1pm at the Arena Pernambuco in Recife. At the time I was not a coffee drinker but had a few cups that morning probably knowing that there will be a lot of stress ahead. I didn't really notice it in the early hours but after breakfast I looked out of the window and there was some heavy rain which got worse from hour to hour. All public transport into Recife seemed to have stopped and no taxis were available either. That was the first moment of a bit of anxiety because we still had to pick up our tickets from a German supporter who only gave us his phone number. We were supposed to meet up at Recife's train station and make our way to the stadium via subway but that plan was for the bin due to the weather conditions and not knowing when to arrive in the city from Olinda which was roughly thirty minutes away.

Suddenly, a small van passed our hostel and a few guys including me followed it quickly and asked the driver if he could drive us to Recife (it was probably a mixture of English, Portuguese and Spanish language). The guy understood and after we offered him some Reais—Brazil's currency—the man drove about six or seven German supporters including me and my buddy to Recife's train station. At that point the rain was a monsoon and a few Germans told us that there are rumours that the match might get called off. After waiting for about thirty to forty-five minutes at the station we decided to make our way to the stadium with about two hours left before kick-off and still no tickets physically in our hands. Before we hopped on the subway there was a bit of a shock moment after a group of people, mainly women, started screaming and jumping to the side before entering the station. For a second I was expecting an attack or assault by someone but it turned out to be a rat who kept jumping around in the rain and in front of the train station. After the incident was cleared we finally made it onto the tube and arrived at the stadium station about forty minutes later. The rain had not really stopped by then and we were relatively far from the stadium still with no tickets in sight and the text message contact with the guy who had our tickets was getting fewer and fewer the closer we approached kick-off. After a shuttle bus drove us about a ten to fifteen minute walk away from the stadium we finally made it to the ground. After one final attempt to pick up our tickets we received a final message from our ticket dude that he was waiting right at the gate to get in with us. By the time I had pretty much lost belief and patience—I had paid the tickets a few months prior to the match—but the guy was in fact in front of the stadium and handed us the tickets. We just arrived with the national anthems and made it on time. A groundhopper's victory in the end!

Our tickets were right in the American end who showed up in decent numbers and with a Dirk Nowitzki jersey I was wearing that day I contributed to the German-American friendship in style.

To have a happy ending to a matchday that could have ended quite badly was surely a personal victory and the journey back to Olinda felt great despite all the stress. The reward was a proper hotel in Recife we booked for the following days and plenty of beers.

I noticed the tension in Brazil when the host nation nearly got knocked out by Chile in the round of the last sixteen with gunshots coming from favelas once again during the penalty shoot-out eventually won by the Brazilians. This match was the first sign that Brazil might not be good enough to win the tournament and ended in a historic defeat in the semi-finals known as the "Mineirazo" (Agony of Mineirão). I had left Brazil prior to that and my last game on Brazilian soil was the round of the last sixteen clash between Argentina and Switzerland which I watched at Rio de Janeiro Airport. At the time I did not know that I would return to the country five years later with my future wife from Minas Gerais.

In February 2019 I got married at Hendon Town Hall in north-west London. Four months later me, my wife and my daughter travelled to Brazil to celebrate with the in-laws and Brazilian friends in the beautiful town of Tiradentes in Minas Gerais some three hours from Belo Horizonte. Minas Gerais is known as the "Stomach of Brazil" due to the excellent homemade food. At the same time in June the Copa América was held in Brazil and it was not coincidental that I had tickets for a few fixtures including Brazil versus Argentina at the Mineirao. When it comes to national team rivalries this is one of the most well-known between two of the most successful football countries in the world including some outstanding football players. I had seen Lionel Messi a few times including that stunning performance for Barcelona at the Champions League final 2011 and it is always great to see him live although this time it was a very physical encounter with Brazil being on top winning 2–0 and some controversial referee decisions involved. There were two things I noticed when I attended this Copa América semi-final in Belo Horizonte. First, there was a lot of banter between the two fan bases and there was no violent tension at all. Clearly, when it comes to club football in South America—compared to national teams—the supporters show much more hatred and in most local derbies away fans are not even allowed anywhere near the stadium.

Secondly, both national teams Brazil and Argentina are not in their best state these days. Brazil had not won a World Cup since 2002 and obviously, the 7–1 defeat at the World Cup 2014 is still a big scar of such a proud football nation. Argentina have not been doing a whole lot better despite the World Cup final in

2014. The constant discussion that Messi can't win a title with his home nation and only with Barcelona is a debate that had an impact on the team and the World Cup 2018 was a rather poor showing by the 'Gauchos'. It subdued the atmosphere a little bit for this big game but still from a groundhopping point of view I loved the experience. The stadium, the pre-match gatherings and simply to be there felt special.

Belo Horizonte is a city that impressed me less than Rio or Salvador but I knew I had to see the Mineirao and due to the fact that my wife is a Cruzeiro supporter from the area I will be back for sure for the local derby against Atlético Mineiro. Stunningly, Cruzeiro recently got relegated to the Serie B for the first time in their club history. A development that occurs more and more often that traditional football clubs with huge fan bases and potential drop one or more leagues. A poor board and management are one major factor that relegation happens to very traditional clubs and other teams with more financial stability take over. Hamburg, Sunderland, Kaiserslautern, Málaga, Leeds United, Cruzeiro and at some point even River Plate experienced it in recent years. And the pandemic of 2020 hit professional football really hard so there will be more clubs to come who might experience a downfall.

The day after Brazil made it to the Copa América final my wife and I flew down to Porto Alegre to see the second semi-final between Chile and Peru. It was held at the Grêmio Arena which is a modern stadium with not a whole lot to do near the stadium. As it was June and hence winter in Brazil, there is one thing that is quite significant about the sheer size of this country: the difference in temperature. In Rio it was still quite humid with around twenty-five degrees which seemed to be cold for the locals as they were running around in winter jackets whereas I was in shorts and a sleeveless top… Belo Horizonte was mild and less muggy with pleasant twenty degrees and then there was Porto Alegre where the temperature dropped to zero in the evening. After a nice couple of hours in a brilliant steakhouse downtown we headed to the stadium and we felt the cold straight away—although, we had our headwear and gloves sorted with us. It was an uninspiring Chile performance and Peru won the game comfortably 3-0. Temperatures would drop even further to below zero as we headed to the beautiful towns of Gramado and Canela in the state of Rio Grande do Sul the day after the match which offered some fine cuisine and some beautiful landscape. It did remind me of the Black Forest and there is a significant German background in the area. Interestingly, the best homemade apple strudel I ever had was served just outside Canela from an old German recipe in a house which is a museum nowadays.

It was a lovely time in the south of Brazil up until the matchday morning of the third place match between Argentina and Chile in São Paulo. I had tickets for the match and we had to arrive at Porto Alegre Airport early to make it on time for the 1pm kick-off at the Corinthians Arena in one of the biggest cities in the world. Unfortunately, what I did not know prior to checking-in was that our airline got bust a few months earlier. I am not sure what happened but I did not get any info on that nor do I remember that their website was updated. Regardless, our flight to São Paulo was cancelled. Luckily it was São Paulo so there were loads of other airlines going pretty much every hour to this major hub. In order to make the kick-off I had to buy two new flight tickets with an immediate departure. After it took ages to purchase these including some decent amount of paperwork we rushed to the gate and departed more or less on time. I had about ninety minutes before the start of the match when we entered the airport in São Paulo to pick up our luggage, throw our bags into our hotel and immediately travel onwards to the Arena Corinthians. The good thing is that most of the taxi drivers who drive me to stadiums world-wide know ways to make it to the stadium faster when I am in a rush. No matter if Edinburgh, Lisbon, Regensburg, Genoa, Buenos Aires or São Paulo taxi drivers always try to get you to the ground on time (taking a few rip-offs in other cities aside). The problem with a city like São Paulo is non-stop traffic and it is not recommended to take the Metro due to safety reasons—at least if you are a gringo—so we did not manage to make kick-off but at least attended large parts of the game. The Arena Corinthians is a lovely architecture and it looked stunning already from the outside. It is in a rough area with more police presence than usual for international games which was probably a good thing because locals spotted me straight away just like in Montevideo or Salvador. I probably just look like a European cash cow to them. I do have my phone with me all the time for pictures which would be incentive enough to get robbed so I had to keep my eyes open although travelling with a Brazilian local made it a very smooth journey anyway and I never carry too much cash or valuables with me.

After a sprint from the taxi to the stadium we had to go through a few police chains by showing our match tickets and then we finally made it into the ground. We had great seats and the atmosphere was lovely. Not because it was so tense, actually it was more tense on the pitch with Messi seeing a straight red and clearly this being a proper rivalry between the two countries. However, as it was the third place match the Chileans and Argentinians fans did not take it too seriously and even more so the majority of Brazilians in the stadium, most of them

Corinthians supporters, mocked both teams for ninety minutes. My wife had to translate everything for me obviously but the atmosphere in our stand was hilarious. It was the moment where I finally calmed down after some stressful hours starting at Porto Alegre Airport and the desperate attempt to make it to the game. Arena Corinthians is a stunning ground and when the sun goes down it shines through an open slot between the stands and the roof with favelas in the background. It was not only an impressive scenery but it also made me realize how lucky I am to be able to attend these fixtures world-wide. Brazil is a tremendous country and very unpredictable I found out a few times which makes it all so interesting. A country with people that deserve so much better than all the poverty, crime and inequality. But sitting there in the sunset of São Paulo with my wife watching Argentina and Chile really summed my life: a never ending journey of discovering football grounds of discovering football grounds in a country I fell in love with and my wife being around all that time—from Rio to Belo Horizonte via Porto Alegre and Gramado and its final destination the huge city of São Paulo. The treat of the evening was sushi at the vibrant Avenida Paulista in a city with a significant Japanese background. After the game, we tried to find a taxi to make it from the stadium back to the city and after we found one all the stress was over and another stadium was added to my list. My wife, the taxi driver and I talked a little about the game and the question came up where I was from as I did not speak Portuguese. After my wife said: 'Germany', the taxi driver turned to her and said: 'From all the men in the world you had to choose a German!' This was the last remark to the hurting 7–1 defeat for the Brazilians and I tried to laugh off his comment. It had been a long day...

Mineirão (July 2019)

Arena do Grêmio (July 2019)

Arena Corinthians (July 2019)

Printed in Great Britain
by Amazon